We Native Americans came from the East

Without tutelage towards the new "land without evil"

Cacildo Marques

ISBN: **978-1727161854**

Cover design: Cacildo Marques, with pictures of Sitting Bull and a Quechua girl from Ecuador

Marques, Cacildo

We Native Americans came from the East/ Cacildo Marques. Maryland, 2018.

126p.

ISBN: **978-1727161854**

1. Social Groups. 2. Indian Groups. I. Title

DDC 306.089

We Native Americans came from the East

Cacildo Marques

ÍNDICE

Preface

I have written this book a little to advocate on my own account, since I am a grandson of an Indian of the Kiriri tribe, but I must remember that I also descended from Semites, Negroes, French and Portuguese, at least. My maternal grandfather was stolen from the jungle at the age of two, and my mother had nothing to learn from him about the life of the tribe, for the Tupi language itself was erased of his memory. There is research showing that 94% of Brazilians are offspring of indigenous people, a number that should be close to that of all of Latin America, so, for self-interest, almost all Latinos in the New World should embrace the cause of the natives.

Of course that people of one ethnic group can engage in the struggle for another ethnicity, such as Ethiopians by Slavs, Eskimos by African pygmies, Gypsies by Celts. But when the near blood circulates in their veins the delivery is certainly more definitive.

The arguments in this book, however, are not tools for raising the native peoples only, but tools for improving the lifestyle of all American peoples. At least, I hope so.

I do not seek here to blame the governments for what they have not done so far, or for what they have done wrong, because the dichotomy between what we want and what we do not want is much more grounded in knowing-ignoring couple than in the good-bad fight. The governments we have, especially Latin Americans, do not produce the quagmire just for the population, but also for themselves. If I know a little and the reader knows a little bit, we can both contribute to increase the knowledge of the leaders.

In front of the Manichaeism that opposes monotheists to idolaters, Jews to Gentiles, Christians to Pagans, Jacobins to Girondins, Catholics to Protestants, Blacks to Whites, Socialists to Individualists, Liberals to Conservatives and Bolsheviks to Mensheviks, we must counterpose the binomial Clarified X Unlettered. What is advantageous in this view is that it is enough to instruct well the ill-informed one so that he becomes enlightened. It is not implicit that the task is easy and quick, once it can require Herculean effort and last for decades and more decades.

For example, one should not have the illusion that with proper words and appropriate examples we will eliminate the color bias in the minds of petrified adult people. Preparing children against prejudice is easy, but for adults it is more practical to teach them to behave like civilized people, while dominating the manifestation of inconvenient feelings, than to take away these antisocial feelings. Thus, between two equally melanophobic people in the stands of a soccer stadium, sitting side by side, one of them may come to scream his low feelings while the other remains in his phlegm, without showing any "racism". The first one is arrested by the police and the second goes home quietly at the end of the game. The difference between the two is that the former, unlike the latter, has received no civilizational training to contain its harmful impulses.

All that has been said above draws a picture of the difficulty that the thesis of the book will encounter. But I do not give up warning and try to get the message to reach the pertinent people. Based on Roger Bacon's ideas, Pierre d'Ailly published in 1410, two years before being appointed cardinal, his work *Imago Mundi*, in which he guaranteed that if someone left the Iberian Peninsula to the West, he would arrive in India. Christopher Columbus read the book and went on a quest for funding for his 1492 voyage (Clegg, Brian, *The First Scientist, The Life of Roger Bacon*, Carrol & Graf Publishers, NY, 2003). As it is known, the truth was not all there, since the author did not count on America in the middle of the road, although the ground of the sphericity of the Earth was correct. But that's how things work, if they have to work. And the Columbus's good luck was not small, for if he had not found America, his fleet would have succumbed about four months after its departure, lost in the Pacific Ocean.

Cacildo Marques, August 2018.

We Native Americans came from the East

Cacildo Marques

1.
Appearances seriously deceive

While arriving in America the Europeans found us naked or half-naked. This brought the idea of freedom and simplicity for some, but of poverty and ignorance for others, who certainly were the majority.

They did not see us as the Far Eastern Asians that we are, but as lost Indians.

Looking closely, anyone realizes that our appearance is much closer to that of the Chinese, Koreans, Vietnamese, Indonesians, Filipinos and Japanese than that of Indians. The motive of the confusion that the Europeans made at the end of the fifteenth century is something clear for the psychology of the present day: they were influenced by their own expectation. They left Europe with the aim of finding a new way for the Indies, since the Muslims had taken Constantinople in 1453 and dominated the traditional passage by the Mediterranean Sea.

If they had found populations of white complexion, Caucasian people, they would have found that they turned around to reach Europe again. If they had found black-skinned people, they would have thought they were on some island in Africa. Since what they found was people whose skin was intermediate in color, between black and white, and what they were looking for were Indians, they had no great doubts: they had reached some point lost in the Indies. Those men on the beach were certainly Indians, that is, they were indigenous people. That was the reading they did and it prevailed for five centuries.

That our phenotype is closer to the individuals of the Far East than to the Indians is a notorious fact today. Two episodes in Brazil illustrate this. In one of them, a Japanese farmer from State of Mato Grosso had a raid with a former employee, towards the end of the twentieth century. One day, this former employee murdered an indigenous man in the area. At the police station he explained why he killed the native: looking from afar, he imagined him to be the Japanese, who was his enemy.

The second case occurred in the city of Sao Paulo. The casting director of the films Taina I and Taina II, that happen in the Amazon having as heroine an indigenous child, Taina, brought the main actress of the story, Eunice Baia, of indigenous family, from Para, to live with her in Sao Paulo, where she would direct the adolescent in studies and encourage her progress in the artistic career. She was once at a restaurant with the girl and met an old acquaintance. Her friend's comment was: "Wow! I did not know you had a Japanese daughter!"

Occupation. How did one settle the East of America?

Native Americans are generally more like Filipinos than like Japanese and Chinese. The closest ones to the Japanese are the Quechua, from Peru and Ecuador, and their Brazilian relatives, the Tupi and the Guarani. The fact that we Brazilians look close to the Quechua, not to the Aymara of Bolivia, for example, is a point in favor of the thesis by General Couto de Magalhaes, in the book The Wild, according to which the natives of northwestern South America went up the Andes and descended eastwards, to populate the Amazon and the coast of Pindorama, today Brazil, a deduction he made from a Tupi song that says: "Let's head east and conquer the land of the palm trees". Land of the palm trees in Tupi is Pindorama, the old name of Brazil.

As the Aztecs, Incas, and remnants of the Mayan cities showed some civilizational progress, the rest of us were still in the pre-agricultural stage, advancing only in handicrafts, with clay, wood, straw and stone, along with efficient hunting and fishing techniques.

Amerigo. What important discovery did Amerigo Vespucci make in 1499?

In 1960 were found remains of houses built by the Norwegian Vikings in northeastern Canada. They arrived around the year 1000, but saw no advantage in colonizing the region and populating it with their people, or had no contingent for the enterprise, as it happened with the Portuguese in the sixteenth century, who circled Australia and went on, for lack of settlers to leave there. After the Norwegians, the Italian from Genoa, Christopher Columbus, came, aided financially by the Spanish crown, dropping anchor in the Bahamas in 1492.

Just as the Portuguese nobleman, the architect of the Treaty of Tordesillas, Duarte Pacheco Pereira, who in 1498 coasted Brazil imagining to be on islands of the Old World, Columbus did not know that he had discovered for the Europeans a new continent, outside Europe, Africa, and the Indian Subcontinent. Who came to the conclusion that the new lands were on a different continent was another Italian, his friend and collaborator, Amerigo Vespucci, who also worked for the Iberian crowns. He sailed along the coast of Venezuela in 1499, officially discovering the mouth of the Amazon River. In 1501 he undertook another voyage, this time being part of the expedition commanded by the Portuguese navigator Goncalo Coelho. He drove in Pernambuco and sailed southward, exploring Bahia, Cabo Frio, Guanabara Bay, the estuary of the River Plate and the coast of Patagonia. In 1507 the German researcher Martin Waldsemuller published in Paris an account of these voyages ("Quatuor Americi Vesputii Navigationes"), using for the first time the word America to refer to the new continent. So, since 1507, we of the New World are all Americans.

Capacity. Why did they see us as inferior?

If we had been seen as Asians from the Far East, we would have been associated with the power of the Yuan Dynasty, initiated by Kublai Khan, grandson of Genghis Khan, whose descendants dominated almost the entire Old World, reaching Iraq and Syria in the centuries immediately preceding of the maritime discoveries. We would have been seen as able people, of science and power, not as inferior people waiting for guardianship.

The paradigm spread throughout the remaining five centuries of the millennium, so that when the pseudotheories of human races arose in the nineteenth century we were not included in the "yellow race", as it would be expected: they created the fourth race to classify us, the red race. It is that since the arrival of the English to North America was given the nickname of red skins to the natives.

Helplessness. Did we have possibility to equal us to the Europeans?

The cities of Tenochtitlan (Mexico City) and Cusco, these advanced nuclei of the Americas, represented two points out of the curve in the immensity of areas of a continent larger than Africa. Throughout the rest of the territory we were helpless, without clothing, without powerful weapons and without antibodies against diseases brought by the Europeans.

The generals of the tribes of the United States were valiant warriors, but fought in vain in defense of the lands that they used, because their advantage in contingent annulled in front of the superior technology of the English.

Not only the possession of superior technology encouraged the settlers against the natives. The biggest incentive was that they thought the red-skinned people were a lower type of person, who did not deserve access to the Old World culture, and would not even be able to absorb it. All of these things would have been very different if all the European immigrants had seen us as the relatives we are of the Chinese, not as a completely exotic type of dismembered Indian.

It is not that Indian should have been seen at the time of the discoveries as inferior to the Asians of the Far East. The problem is that this was the reality. They saw a people of very old culture with great delay as for the new techniques of navigation and war. Portuguese settled colonies in several areas of India and pretended to dominate the whole territory, not achieving such feat for lack of contingent. Later British came and colonized the country, including the neighboring areas that include Bangladesh, Pakistan and the land of Buda, Nepal. They respected only some Portuguese colonies, like Goa, Daman and Diu.

As for China and Japan, Portuguese warriors knew there was no chance. With the exception of the small Chinese area of Macau, which has belonged to Portugal for centuries, the cultural penetration that occurred in those two countries occurred through missions of Catholic clerics.

Montezuma. How did the Europeans treat the emperor?

In Mexico, it is reported that Hernan Cortez made friends with Emperor ("Tlatoani") Montezuma II the Young (Montezuma = "Snake of Obsidian"), or Montezuma Xocoyotzin, born in 1466 and exercising power from 1502, when in 1519 arrived in the capital Tenochtitlan, now Mexico City, intending to do business, trading the gold of the American people for European manufactured goods. He also wanted to do cultural exchanges. But in one of his absences, on a voyage of exploration for a few months, his soldiers whipped the natives, trying to impose Christianity in the least recommendable way: breaking the totems, which were the representation of their idols. We do not know if before that they had the shocking information that for these idols the Aztecs sacrificed children, what would help, without justifying the act, to explain the indignation. When Cortez returned, he found the two groups in the middle of the war, choosing to stay on the side of his people, Europeans. Montezuma died in 1520, murdered by Spaniards or, according to the most current version in present-day Mexico, sacrificed by the Aztecs themselves for being credulous and weak in the face of the European invaders. Since then, the chance of peaceful coexistence between natives and conquerors of the Old World has disappeared in the area of Spanish colonization of North America for a long time.

Emperor Montezuma Xocoyotzin

It did not help in the solution of the conflict that Cortez had as his mistress Malinche (named Malinalli in his native language and baptized as Marina), born in 1496 in the Nahua ethnic group of the coast, an excellent interpreter who spoke three languages - Mayan,

Aztec, and, later, Spanish -, had a child with him, but could not be his wife, since he was married in Spain. He arranged for her then a marriage with Juan Xamarillo, and with this husband she had a daughter. Mother of the two mestizos, Malinche is considered by many as "the mother of the Mexican nation". Others see her as a traitor, who with her abilities helped Europeans to dominate the native Mexicans. He died in 1551.

Cuauhtemoc. Did the successor have better luck?

The successor of Montezuma II was Emperor Cuauhtemoc ("Eagle Who Landed"), his nephew, who in that year of 1520 tried to fortify the city and reorganize the army to face the Spanish, who had been expelled, but were expected back, bringing reinforcements. The father of Montezuma II, Montezuma I, was born in 1398, and reigned from 1440 until his death in 1469. These monarchs attended schools, but we must understand by pre-Columbian "schools" in America not the Pythagorean institution, destined to the formation of young men in general, but training courses for technicians and leaders, as there was in Sumerian civilization during the time of Emperor Hamnurabi (eighteenth century BC) from Babylon.

In fact, Cortez returned in 1521 and kept the city under siege for three months. On August 13, his troops captured the emperor, who had escaped to the city of Tlatelolco, where he had previously been governor, in what he made a bad choice, with the abandonment of the empire's capital. In a letter to King Charles I of Spain, Cortez reported that Cuauhtemoc pointed his dagger at his waist and told him to kill him with that weapon, because he had been unable to defend his people. Cortez, however, who had received a canoe full of pieces made of gold, wanted more, and decided not to kill the emperor. He preferred to subject him and other prisoners to torture, with the burning of his feet and other punishments, to tell them where to find more gold. On a trip to Honduras, he took the emperor along to show other native rulers that he was the master of the situation. Two of Cortez's auxiliaries revealed at one point that Cuauhtemoc was conspiring with other emperors, those from Texcoco and Tlacopan, to kill him. Finally, on February 26, 1525, after being interrogated, Cortez ordered he was hanged, as an example against anyone who could attack his life. He was the last Aztec emperor to have been sworn in without the blessing of the Spaniards. Bernal Diaz del Castillo, a man of letters who accompanied Cortez, wrote in the book "The True History of the Conquest of New Spain" that the execution was unfair and that Cortez started to suffer insomnia, out of remorse.

Mixing. Are we Afro-Amerindians more indigenous or more mestizos?

Proportionally, we are very few indigenous today without miscegenation with Europeans, Semites or Africans. As the voyagers of the explorers came across the Atlantic, the less amalgamated Indians are more to the west. The further one goes east, in any part of the continent, the more miscegenation there is.

After much mixing, we are now American-Jews, American-Afro, American-British, American-Iberian and so on. We must be grateful to heaven for sharing the culture of these Old World peoples in our genes. But we must not forget that our original continental culture is of people from Asian origin, from the Far East.

Mixed with the Europeans, especially Jews and Christians, we received formation focused on forgiveness and rejection of the law of retaliation (*lex talionis*). We did not have this here, as did the Filipinos, Indonesians, Koreans, Vietnamese, Chinese, and Japanese until centuries ago. We lived in wars of honor, tribes against tribes, because that was the dictation of those times. Having warred so much did not make us any stupider, because that was part of the human evolution.

At the beginning of the 21st century we reached the stage of an America without wars, after the agreement that ended the guerrilla of Colombia in 2017. After an Western Europe without wars, with the end of the Balkan conflict in 1995, we also have an America without wars, from the northern tip of Canada to Tierra del Fuego.

2.
Darwinian Speciation

By the middle of 2017, and since many years before, the consensus on the date of Homo sapiens' arrival in America was that this was twelve thousand years ago. The less credulous believed in eight thousand years, always based on records in caverns. In the second half of 2017, researchers concluded that the human presence in America is thirty thousand years old, based on material collected in the State of Mato Grosso, Brazil. A confirmation of these measurements is necessary, perhaps an *experimentum crucis*, before the yaw represented by the finding.

Pioneers. Since when are we in America?

The Tupi, and consequently the Guarani and other minor ethnic groups, arrived in the easternmost part of the continent, which is now the Brazilian coast, three thousand years ago, half a millennium after the Sumerians invented writing in its cuneiform form, and the Egyptians created the hieroglyphs.

The Tupi were not the first humans to reach the region that is now Brazil. In the 1990s it was discovered in Lagoa Santa, State of Minas Gerais, what for a long time was considered the oldest skull in the Americas, dating to 11,500 years (unfortunately destroyed in the fire of the National Museum of Brazil on September 2, 2018). It belongs to a young woman of approximately 20 years, that the researcher Walter Neves, of the University of Sao Paulo (USP), baptized of Luzia, in reference to the fossil of Lucy, of Tanzania. A few years later, skeletons of the same era and similar in appearance were identified in other South American countries. More recently, a skeleton was discovered in the Yucatan peninsula, in Mexico, which scientists think is the oldest, twelve thousand years old, of a young girl of about 16 years, whom the researchers named Naia.

Luzia, who lived in Brazil five thousand years before the arrival of the Tupi, did not look like Asian, but African, what intrigued the researchers very much.

There must have been a wave of migration to South America eleven or twelve thousand years ago, most likely across the Behring Strait, as it did later with the Asians. Twelve thousand years ago there is maybe no possibility of a population with the appearance of the Mongols having yet been formed. The migrants of that time were therefore African families who traveled to the Far East and from there they reached the Americas. They may also have come from Antarctica, or through Atlantic islands that no longer exist.

If it is hypothesized that there are populations living in the Americas among ten thousand and twelve thousand years ago, it is almost certain that they died out, and the migratory wave of people who "rose" from China and crossed the Strait of Behring appeared millennia after first wave. If not completely extinct, few remaining copies may have been mixed with newly arrived populations from the Far East. Currently DNA samples are being examined of Luzia contemporaries, collected in Lagoa Santa, which will soon bring surprises.

Archaeological sites in Central America attest to the indigenous occupation dating to 6,500 years. We came from the Far East certainly at this stage.

Differences. What kinship is there between the tribes of north and south?

The natives of the United States and Canada have a very different appearance from that of the Aztecs, who are more like those of South America. The Eskimos, who are more similar to the Chinese in terms of physiognomy, are more distant, from the body, of the peoples of the Americas and East Asia, at least as far as stature is concerned. They have been isolated for millennia from the southern peoples. And the differences between the peoples of the United States and those of Mexico are certainly due to the barrier represented by the Great River, or Rio Grande. If for the contemporary people and for the Spanish colonizers the river does not bring any impediment, for the ancients, even for mystical reasons, it constituted itself in factor of separation.

By the phenomenon of speciation, of the theory of evolution, the differences have accentuated over the centuries and millennia. A

Sioux man showed no sign of being close relative of a Guarani of Paraguay, although they both had the same skin color. This difference helped to cement the unfounded belief that we were Indians, from India.

However, without the bias of the expectation that here it was a lost piece of India, an Old World traveler who had had contact here with Guarani, Tupi, Inca, Aztec, Navajo, Sioux, and Eskimo, for example, an Arab, and had been asked to construct the spoken picture of the type of man he saw here, he would come to a Mongoloid face, not an Indian face.

The Europeans who came to paint us, differently, made portraits of Indians, who, in fact, did not exist on this continent. They came with an image in their mind, and they could not escape it.

The difference between the treatment of Native Americans by the English in North America and the Iberians in Central and South America comes basically from the fact that the Iberians who came to America were Jews and Moors or their descendants mixed with European countries.

While in North America many wars led to the almost extinction of native tribes, in the area of Iberian colonization, further south, Europeans married "Indian" people, creating large mixed populations.

In the western most part of the Brazilian Amazon there are many cities formed by entirely native populations. On the coast of the country, all municipalities are mixed, with Guarani villages without mixing only on the coast of the State of Sao Paulo, since the great development of the region occurred in the Plateau of Piratininga. In the 1970s, with the creation of the Rio-Santos Highway, several tribes living in the area of extractive and fishing had, for the first time, contact with the so-called "whites" since the wars of the "Tamoios Confederation".

At the beginning of the twentieth century, differently, there were still many tribes unmixed with people of European origin scattered throughout the States of Minas Gerais, Bahia, Espirito Santo, and also by Northeastern states. The advance of urbanization in these areas, especially between the thirties and seventies, caused all these peoples to merge and lose their native language. Indigenous tribes at the beginning of the 21st century are found on the coast of Sao Paulo, in the west of Parana, or in the interior of the States of Goias, Tocantins, Para and areas more to the west of Brazil. Tribes that were reorganized in Bahia, Pernambuco, Maranhao, or other coastal states are, in general, groupings of mestizos, formerly called "caboclos". Almost all of them are bearded and have no knowledge of the language of their ancestors.

3.
Our Legacy

The first Europeans in the Americas did not take to their continent only gold, precious stones and vegetable riches, as was their purpose. They also took what they could absorb from the culture of the natives, if not exemplary of these populations, as it was the case of the young Pocahontas.

Certainly the greatest covetousness fell on gold, but many other products gained space on vessels returning to Europe.

Learning. What have they learned from us?

From the native culture they took positive things and also troubles, which they considered innocent items, like the habit of smoking. It is notorious that the habit of bathing the whole body, within rivers, lakes and the sea, was taken from here. Europeans bathed with the use of tubs, while watering towels and passing over parts of the body, as an inheritance of medieval Catholicism, which condemned the public baths in the fountains (pools) of Ancient Rome.

Thomas Morus imagined the account of a Portuguese navigator who, returning to Europe, described an island, very developed for the time, in which the system of common property, very similar to that experienced by the Christians of the first three centuries, worked satisfactorily. On the farms, he said, there was a machine for hatching eggs, a brooder, which greatly improved poultry production. The name of this fantastic island was Utopia, or "no place", in Greek. The book, *The Utopia*, was published in 1516.

This beneficial inspiration which the New World exercised in Europeans had a reverse response one century later in the work of Thomas Hobbes, *The Leviathan*, and, decades later, in Jonathan Swift's, *Gulliver's Travels*. What Gulliver saw in his navigations were examples of extreme inequalities between human beings, while Hobbes in his philosophy had described man as the wolf of man.

Distortion. Is our legacy well understood?

Again another compatriot of those three Englishmen, Anthony Ashley-Cooper, the third Earl of Shaftesbury, resumed a line apparently related to that of Thomas Morus, despite being a man of the Conservative Whig party. Shaftesbury launched, as the basis of his philosophy, the belief in man's natural benevolence. This view, blatantly contrary to Christian preaching, the basis of Morus, according to which it is necessary to plant the seed of the "word of salvation", which has difficulty thriving on stony ground, has generated very problematic sectarian currents, based on the lie. It was certainly not a positive inspiration derived from the natives of the New World, who lived in constant wars.

And the wars took place for the simple fact that human evolution has no way to burn stages. If the Europeans, literate and dominators of the metallurgical arts, were frequently living in war, the natives of the Americas did so much better.

Certainly it was never Thomas Morus' intention to conceal the New World war stage, but the romantics who came later abused the lying strategy that presented the savage man as kind and absolutely peaceful. Peace the world always wanted it, but the desire could not overcome the limitation imposed by the incipient civilizing stage.

Morus was far from being the pioneer of Romanticism, for the Island of Utopia was not a country of savages. He was inspired by reports of the absence of private property among New World natives, who shared the forests for extractive and hunting, and the rivers and seas for fishing, navigation and bathing. He then transported this configuration to a very civilized, technologically advanced island, but preserving the condition of common property. As much he knew that the situation was fanciful that baptized the country of "no place".

If in Thomas Morus the place is what was fanciful, in romantic writers, apologists of the good savage, that type of individual they imagined, telluric, peaceful, tolerant and benevolent, is who was fanciful.

If we have a vein for pacifism, it is the same as that of the Europeans, the present Africans and the Asians, and it will not put the cart before the horse. Just as the Western European did not have peace before 2005 ("Bosnian War"), neither did we. If Western Europeans defend peace at all costs since then, we will also do so from 2017 (end of the "Revolutionary Armed Forces of Colombia" guerrilla warfare), unless insanity insists on retaking the past of long-term dictatorships, with its inherent conflicts.

Just as in the twentieth century they misrepresented John Maynard Keynes's ideas, changing the investment project to obtain and maintain full employment for the one of "intervention" to quell crisis, and Maria Montessori's ideas, replacing the model of substituting the elementary teacher in classroom, this one supplied with appropriate didactic material (analogical), by a scheme in which the teacher was called a "guide" and continued in the classroom (teacher would have to work outside the classroom, as an examiner), of the same way they disfigured the ideas of Thomas Morus, who imagined a civilized people who attained peace exactly by its high stage of progress and had almost two centuries later his work as inspiring a doctrine that sees the wild man as the bearer of "natural goodness".

4.
Pre-Columbian development

Positive visions of the native peoples of the Americas have always been relegated to the dust of drawers. The Brazilian Patriarch of Independence, Jose Bonifacio de Andrada e Silva, for example, had plans to install primary schools in all "indigenous" villages, and to develop agriculture in those communities, with official support ("Projects for Brazil"). None of this was done, because the agents who could put the idea into practice were taken from prejudice, fueled by the paradigm of the "lost Indian". Only in the twenty-first century, by the dynamics of time and commitment of some selfless, in a slow work, schools have reached the villages scattered throughout the country.

Arithmetic. How did we see the numbers in 1500?

The inhabitants of most of the Brazilian villages, when the Europeans arrived, counted up to three, nominally, identifying the number four with the collective. They said, in their tongues: one, two, three, many. In Tupi, jepeh, moukoin, mosapyr, irundyc. The novice Jose de Anchieta, in the school he created with Father Manoel da Nobrega in the Plateau of Piratininga, in order to alphabetize the Tupi children, introduced expression for number five and, from it, for other larger numbers. He said "che po", my hand, to five (he preferred the letter "x" instead of "ch", "xe" instead of "che", since in Latin the "ch" remits to "k"; Professor Eduardo Navarro writes "se", with "pu" for hand, which gives "se pu"; the letter "y" in Tupi-Guarani is pronounced like the French "u", but in a guttural way; Tupi and Guarani are very close languages, sharing almost all of the vocabulary and grammatical rules, resulting in fusion in the Tupi-Guarani language, which Anchieta, more based on the various Tupi phrases, called *neengatu*, good language, or general language).

The number ten, according to Anchieta, was written as "moukoin po", two hands, while the number twenty was said "che po che py", my hands and my feet.

From six to ten the numbers look like this:

che po jepeh
che po moukoin
che po mosapyr
che po irundyc
moukoin po

Counting from eleven to twenty was the same resource: moukoin po jepeh, moukoin po moukoin, moukoin po mosapyr, etc.

The Jesuits of the Seven Peoples of the Missions, from the extreme-south of Brazil to the north of Argentina and the east of Paraguay, followed, decades later, the same orientation for writing and pronunciation of numbers.

This very rudimentary scientific stage was not unique in the Americas, but it was the condition of the people of the countryside, that is, of the jungle. Peoples of the city, restricted basically to some remaining Mayan settlements, to the Aztecs of Mexico and to the Incas of Cusco, Peru, were in another pattern of development.

All the villages of the Americas would be on the same high level of living if the benefits of urbanization and progress had been spread across the continent. The natives "of the jungle" were in the situation of "one, two, three, many" not because they were inferior to any other peoples, but because they were still in a country condition, without communication with the developed brothers of the boroughs.

The Maya, who also reached a high stage of development, were dismantled as an empire when Columbus arrived in America, almost certainly by military defeats in front of the Toltecs, in the ninth century. The few cities still existing were small and were dominated little by little by the Spaniards. But the two cities that served as capitals of Mexico and Peru at that time show that the Americas were not only at the wild stage. The Aztecs, of Emperor Montezuma II, had inherited the advances made by the Mayan people, which historians deduce to have consolidated between the year 2000 BC, with agriculture, and 250 AD, when the practices of hieroglyphic writing, Architecture, Handicraft, Astronomy, Music, Arithmetic and Ecology were already well advanced.

It was disclosed at the beginning of the 21st century that the

Maya recorded the date of the end of the world as being December 20, 2012. The date actually exists, but the interpretation that represented the end of the world stemmed from two human weaknesses: sensationalism and poor reading. Dorion Sagan, son of the cosmologist Carl Sagan and researcher of Mayan documents and monuments, says that the date refers to the beginning of a cycle, representing great renewal for humanity. This ethnicity is not today confined to a territory and with an easily identifiable phenotype, but it is spread over large areas, mainly in Mexico, Central America and the South of the United States, in the chromosomes and in the blood of those who are mixed with the natives of this region.

Zero. Is it true that we used in that time a symbol for zero?

In a communication made in the year 2012, Dorion Sagan said that in the monument of Kobah, Peninsula of Yucatan, is written a date that means the oldest time already registered anywhere in the world. It is a number composed of ten thirteens and four zeros and represents a trillion years before the 14 billion years that astronomers estimate to be the age of the universe.

Zeros? Yes. At the time of the year 250 BC the Maya used a symbol for zero, the cardinality of the empty set. Whereas the Indians, centuries later, came to represent zero in the form of a standing egg, the so-called "goose egg", the Mayans represented it as a lying ellipse in the form of a cocoa bean. There is a not inconsiderable possibility that the Mayans were the first people of the world to write the representation of zero as a positional value, and with a specific symbol.

The numbering system was base 20, representing the toes and hands, but counting was recycled every five, fingers number of the hand, as did Jose de Anchieta in developing the numbering for the children of the School Patio, on the Plateau of Piratininga. There is, therefore, some chance of having there been a partnership in this construction, with the students showing that they used their hands to do approximate counts and with the novice taking advantage of the idea to count each of the natural numbers one by one.

For Mayans, the zero was the almond lying down, which also resembled a current rugby ball. The number 1 was a dot, the 2 was formed by two lying dots, the 3 was formed by three dots - as in the ellipsis symbol - and the 4 was a succession of four points. The first quintet was then completed on the next number, and it, the 5, had no dots, but was represented by a large rod.

The next natural number was the dash with a dot on top, the *che po jepeh* (my hand plus one) from the Anchieta's students. The 7 was, logically, the dash with two points on top. The 10 were two dashes lying down, as in the equal sign, and the 11 were those two dashes with a dot on top of them. The number 15 was three horizontal dashes, and with the dots on them, it was up to the 19. At that time the idea of base 20 was configured: the number 20 was written as a zero, the almond lying down, and a dot written above, but at a distance that would leave the span for the succession dots from there, since 21 was a point (not the almond) with that dot on top, 22 was two points (from number two) with that point above, and so on. One can see that the point on the zero, slightly away from it, corresponds to our digit 2, which is written before zero to form the number 20. The number 31 were two dashes below (10) with a point on top, which completed 11, topped by the highest point representing the 2 of the base 20. When it was 40, the zero was used again at the base, and two points above, with the safe distance to show that they represented two twenties. The number 100 was a dash on top, representing five twenties, with the positional zero underneath.

Already the old Tupi-Guarani language did not have a specific word for the numeral zero, but had the word *aani*, which means "nothing", or "no", and could be used with that meaning.

Taxation. Was there a tax practice already?

Mayan society was theocratic and polytheistic. Political, military, and clerical authorities in the cities were regarded as representatives of the gods on Earth, and rural dwellers, often farmers, paid heavy taxes to support city dwellers.

Mayans did not establish any federative organization between the cities, except in the late period, by external influence, when they tried a confederation. The political model, then, was that of isolated city-states.

Trade. How did the Mayans make transactions?

In addition to Arithmetic, they cultivated Astronomy, Geometry, Architecture, Handicrafts, Culinary, Ecology and Commerce. The study of Astronomy allowed the preparation of the calendar, with the 365 days a year. As an example of Architecture, the pyramids remained, which were built for religious purposes. In the Handicraft the tissues and their dyes are highlighted. In the scope of Ecology, the respect they had for the forests was outstanding. And Commerce was practiced between the Mayan cities themselves and also with other peoples of Central America and Mexico. The cocoa seed, which represented zero in writing, was also used as a coin.

Incas. How were the Incas in the matter of numbers?

In South America, the Incas reached a stage of development close to that of the Maya, which is still demonstrated today by their Architecture. They also developed two numbering systems, one on base 20, another on base 8. However, they did not invent or import writing. If the Tupi and other peoples of Eastern America actually came from Quechua branches, they could not have brought that inheritance.

The Quechua are Andean peoples who had as a common trait the Quechua language. The Incas were part of this culture, as Huancas, Chancas and others also were. The language was spoken from northern Argentina to southern Colombia, and is still widely cultivated today, mainly in Peru. As it had no written form, it was up to the Jesuits to construct its spelling, with a certain unification, as it happened with the Tupi-Guarani in Brazil, to use it in the works of catechization.

Node. How were the numbers represented?

The Inca numerals were not represented by dashes or dots, as the Maya did. The representation was knots given in strings. A single knot was obviously the number 1. Two contiguous knots meant the number 2, and so on. With the number of knots and a representation by color, they could represent values in the order of thousands and even millions. Without the invention or adoption of writing, we were, in South America, at a very late stage of development in front of our Mayan relatives.

The Incas, by mastery of numbers, had advanced knowledge of Astronomy, with the year of 365 days and division of the year in 12 months. But it was not possible for the Spanish settlers to study this knowledge more deeply, since, unlike the case of the Maya cities, there was no written record.

Music. What kind of music was made here?

Music also reached a high stage of development in these pre-Columbian cultures. The Aztecs used drums, made of hollow wood and feline skins, various types of flute and also the *ocarina*, a blowing instrument measuring a little more than five centimeters in diameter, shaped like a long mango, full of holes, and with a beak where the performer blows.

Among the Maya, songs and musical accompaniment were of great importance in religious rituals. They used as instruments the *tunkul*, the ocarina, the snails, the drums and the flutes of bamboo and bone, among others.

The Incas cultivated Music in the affective, warlike, agricultural and funeral expressions. They used five musical notes (corresponding to C, D, F, G and A) instead of our seven notes today. Among their musical instruments, made of wood, bone and clay, the flutes *quena* and *penkullo*, the marine snail *fotuto*, the *antara*, which was a set of united flutes, and the drums *tin* and *wankar* stand out.

The ancient Chinese used five musical notes, with only one difference from the scale of the Incas: instead of lacking the B and the E, of our present scale, the Chinese lack the B and the F. The Chinese, therefore, had the E and the Incas had the next note, half a point above, which was the F, but did not have the E. This difference of only half a point in one of the five used notes was what distinguished the musical notes system of the ancient Chinese from those of their Inca descendants. This does not happen to be a proof of kinship, but it is a fact that reinforces the argument in favor of the identity of blood between the two peoples. Music is a very ancient discipline among the various cultures of the world, and precedes the graphic record very much. Large human collective ventures were carried out with their agents using singing as a means of lightening the weight of the action. For example, if the ancient Egyptians built the pyramids without being subjected to the whip, then, almost certainly, they did that by singing. The Incas used songs of war and agricultural songs, among their four types of song. They are, in one way or another, songs of collective work.

Prejudice. How did the settlers treat us?

If in Mexico between the subjects of Montezuma II and the soldiers of Cortez the conflict did not have happened, a conflict that unleashed the numerous wars that followed between the Spaniards and the natives, accompanied by the even more brutal wars between the English and the natives of North America, certainly the trade to be established between Americans and Europeans would have led to an outbreak of mutual enrichment, with great gains for both sides. The dictates of the time, from the beginning of the sixteenth century, however, took on another type of attitude, which was that of domination by arms. Under the view that we were straying Indians, not descendants of peoples of the Far East, the understanding that we were inferior peoples, while waiting to be subjected to tutelage, slavery, confinement or decimation, was consolidated.

Counties. Are indigenous communities still ignored?

It is only now, at the beginning of the 21st century, by the route of the carriage itself, in the process of expansion of progress, that the "indigenous" people of the Amazon, in several previously inhospitable and lost regions, have their public primary schools and receive education comparable to children of the capitals of the states. Only now the Jose Bonifacio's project of schooling the tribes in the farthest corners is put into practice, not by strategic national effort, as he intended, but by the so-called "ant work", with small municipalities raising resources and fighting to bring to their citizens the benefits of big cities.

In order not to be unfair to Herculean figures of politics, we must recognize here that, in the Brazilian case, the effort is based on a project come from the pen of the genius of Senator Darcy Ribeiro, the Fundef (Fundamental Education Development Fund), which determined the distribution of federal funds specific to municipal education, according to the implicit aspiration of Anisio Teixeira, that the municipality was in charge of primary education. The following government after the implementation of the measure diluted the purpose of the fund, extending it to preschool and high school, under the name of Fundeb (Basic Education Development Fund). But the essence of Darcy Ribeiro's idea remains.

Federation. Where does the idea of federation come from?

That organization of the Maya, which was based on isolated cities, though of the same culture, is in our DNA. We Americans struggle to strengthen the municipalities, each exploiting its potential. Obviously, in isolation, acting on the "every man for himself" scheme, we are left at the mercy of greater forces. Thus, unlike the Mayans, we cannot afford to strengthen our federations as well. But we cannot lose sight of Thomas Jefferson's perspective: federation is the union of federated entities for strategic purposes, not the centripetal force of uniformity. Whatever can be managed with advantage by the municipality, as it is the example of the primary education, so must be done. Are our city councils true parliaments? Are our mayors real chiefs of State? There is no problem in that, quite the opposite. Only we should not harbor illusions that we will survive without federation, without the strength of the union of municipalities and provinces.

And, in this way, we must always be vigilant so that the atrophy of the federation does not occur. It can come in many ways, but the most effective ones come under the aegis of dictatorship or presidentialism of direct election. In both cases, the union falls under a central head who surpasses the local hegemony of the municipal and state chiefs. It is important that in one federation the seigniorage of the currency is submitted to that general head, as well as the army, and that a common language be spoken in all the member states. But we have to resist to demands that have as their aim the nullification of the autonomy of local powers. For example, the ingenious project of Senator Darcy Ribeiro, creating the Fundef, for the education of children, soon generated perverse by-products, as was the creation in 2003 of the Ministry of Cities, which is responsible for paving the streets, channeling streams and various other municipal tasks, passing over governors and mayors. In order to prove the authoritarian and deformed bias of the organ, except for two periods of a few months, its command was under staff of the party of the dictatorship, theoretically closed in 1985. In addition to unreasonably burdening the budget of the Union, the action of that deck puts under its tutelage the local executives, leading them to the intensification of the practice of flattery.

In no time we can conclude that Darcy Ribeiro was wrong to create his project, because he could not foresee the misuse that others would do just that mechanism, by emulating it in situations outside of public education and health services.

Another thrust, not yet implemented, perhaps because it has not been successful in the United States, is the only tax proposal, which plays all taxes on account of one, under the Union control. Lawmakers who defend it as well as the author of the idea, economist Henry George (1839-1897), Pennsylvania, did not realize that such an institute would be used by fascism, or other dictatorial power plan, to implement its unitary State project under undisputed command of a central chief.

If money management is to be left to the Leviathan, that is, to the Union, the use of money must be decentralized so that freedom is always oxygenated. It is not the fact of distributing tax revenues in three levels of power that generates tax oppression or corruption, but the fact that there are serious errors in the conception of the tax design, basically resulting from the ignorance on the theory of proportions. A federative union, after all, should neither institute federal tax, but be served with portions of the tax pie of its federated units, as it happens with the UN.

The federation, as a strategic and progressive instrument, must be defended as an American creation. The ancient Greeks united for defense purposes, as it was the case with the League of Delos, but the ancient peoples failed to consolidate any federative government. The Holy Roman Empire, begun at the coronation of Charlemagne at Christmas of the year 800 and dissolved in 1806, had the role of uniting Christianity under the same monarch, but was never a federal government, so that the subjects of the interior of the majority of the involved regions spent all their lives unaware of the existence of this league.

Under Jefferson's conception, then tempered with the administrative ideas of the Caribbean Alexander Hamilton, the United States federation inspired in the nineteenth century the Italian and Prussian unifications and, in the twentieth century, the Russian Federation and the European Union, which is in the process of consolidation in the 21st century. Before that, it had already served as a model for the formation of the United States of Mexico and the United States of Brazil, which in 1967 was renamed the Federative Republic of Brazil.

The federative idea does not come from the mind of an emperor who wants to dismember his domains in order to facilitate governance. An absolute emperor divides in order to better impose his wills. But the federation, in its American, "Amerindian", construction, has a contrary meaning: States are joined to strengthen themselves, but they preserve their autonomy to the limit of the rupture, which, moreover, is never desirable.

5.
The Plateau of Piratininga

At a date without consensus among historians, but between 1510 and 1515, the Portuguese navigator Joao Ramalho was saved from a shipwreck on the coast of the Captaincy of Sao Vicente. He was hosted by a young chief, Pikeroby ("Little Green Fish"), younger brother of Chief Tibiriça ("Watch-Guard of the Mountain"), a leader who would strongly mark Brazilian history. Going up to the Plateau, Joao Ramalho joined the firstborn daughter of Tibiriça, Mbicy ("Toast"), who was known among the Portuguese as Bartira and was baptized as Isabel (Elizabeth). The wife of Tibiriça was called Potyra ("flower"), from who it comes the attempt to call her daughter also by the same name, albeit with modified pronunciation. Married in Portugal with Catarina Fernandes das Vacas, Ramalho never considered returning to his country of origin, which makes the scholars distrust that he came as a degredado (banned). Here, he held the positions of councilman, captain and mayor, and died in 1580, in the Paraiba Valley.

Another Portuguese navigator, brought along with Joao Ramalho, Antonio Rodrigues, was also welcomed by Pikeroby, who, like his brother Tibiriça, became the father-in-law of an immigrant, marrying to Antonio one of his daughters, later baptized by the Jesuits as Antonia Rodrigues. Another daughter he married with another immigrant who came later, Cosme Fernandes.

Village. The Sao Vicente Village was well accepted in the beginning?

Pikeroby was chief of the Guaianas tribe, of Ururahy, current district of Sao Miguel Paulista, municipality of Sao Paulo. Another brother, Caiuby, went down the Tiete River to climb the Jurubatuba River, today the Pinheiros River, and established a village in the region, becoming chief of those people. Years later, the Jesuits created the Pinheiros Village as a new nucleus of literacy and catechization of native children, after the initial unit of the School Patio, in the town of Piratininga, founded in 1554 with the support of

Chief Tibiriça. Long before that, Martim Afonso de Sousa, donee of the captaincy, officialized in 1530 the Sao Vicente Village, on the coast.

Tibiriça and Caiuby continued to live well with the few Portuguese they knew, but Pikeroby saw the creation of the village on the coast as a threat. In 1534 he organized an attack on Sao Vicente Village and defeated the few soldiers left there by Martim Afonso de Sousa. The village was looted and almost demolished.

Siege. Sao Paulo had better luck at this time?

In 1562 Pikeroby carried out another attack, now of greater proportions, but not on the coast. He joined his son Jaguanharoh ("Brave Jaguar"), who headed a large tribe in the Paraíba Valley, and attacked, for five days, both Pinheiros Village and Sao Paulo of Piratininga. Jesuit Jose de Anchieta recorded that "it was by the mercy of God" that the catechized natives and their relatives turned their hearts to the salvation of the community, many of them responding bravely to the attacks of Pikeroby and Jaguanharoh. Finally, on the fifth day of battle, Jaguanharoh attempted to smash the door of the Church of the School Patio, where women and children of the village had taken refuge, when he was surprised and killed by his own uncle, leader of the place, Chief Tibiriça. The invaders were then defeated. Antonio Rodrigues, Pikeroby's son-in-law, after much talk, managed to convince the rebel chieftain to seal the peace with his brothers. Pikeroby died months later, that same year, 1562.

The Jesuits were then able to resume their work of educating children, forming the generations that constituted the initial pillar of the city of Sao Paulo, which at the beginning of the twenty-first century has more than 12 million inhabitants, surrounded by several conurbated cities where other 11 million live.

6.
The Reductions

The project of evangelization of the natives of southern Brazil and neighboring areas of Argentina and Paraguay, with units also in Uruguay and Bolivia, carried out by the missionaries of the Society of Jesus, the Jesuit Fathers, lasted a little less than a century and a half. The work began in 1609, ending in 1756.

At that time, these lands belonged to the Province of Paraguay, of the Spanish crown, which scaled these priests to bring to the "Indians" the Christian doctrine, with the aim of approximating the inhabitants of the colony to the culture of the European colonizer. As we know, the Portuguese and Spanish crowns were cast from 1580 to 1640.

As it was already done in Sao Paulo de Piratininga half a century ago, the doctrine was transmitted in the language of the natives. For the Missions, or Reductions, this language was the Guarani, today cultivated in Paraguay as Guarani Jopara ("Jopara" = mixed), because of the addition of Hispanic words.

Beginning. How did the introduction of the Catholic Missions take place?

The first Reduction, of 1609, was installed in San Ignacio Guazu, in Paraguay. In the region that today is Argentina, province of Misiones, the Reduction of Our Lady of Loreto was founded as soon as in 1610. On the side that today belongs to Brazil, the Rio Grande of Sao Pedro, now the State of Rio Grande do Sul, in the region of Tape, some nuclei were founded, with San Miguel being the most important. In 1641, shortly after the end of the merger between the Spanish and Portuguese crowns, the Battle of M'Borore took place, between the Guarani and the Bandeirantes who went from Sao Paulo to that area, seeking to enslave the already literate natives, who, thus, were more valuable. The natives, led by the leader Inacio Abiaru, defeated the Bandeirantes, who were headed by Jeronimo Pedroso de Barros, son of Amador Bueno, "The Acclaimed" (he was acclaimed King of Sao Paulo by the population in 1641 without having, however, accepted the crown), but with many casualties, the Guarani and Jesuits decided to migrate, transferring their residences to the west side of the Uruguay River, joining Reductions of the region that today belongs to Argentina.

During the period of the fusion of the crowns, called in the Lusophone area of "Spanish dominion", the Bandeirantes took advantage of the obsolescence of the *Treaty of Tordesillas*, signed in the city of the same name in 1494 and that divided the lands between Portugal and Spain when they were distinct governments, and went to the west, founding numerous settlements in the area that formerly belonged to Spain and which was closed to the penetration of settlers of Portuguese origin. In attempting the same onslaughts in the south, they were faced with a recent civilization, that of the Jesuit Missions. These relentless pioneers thrashed the woods in search of gold and precious stones, creating villages and trails for hundreds of leagues in the south, east, and west. The sweetened manuals of History of Brazil emphasize this aspect and almost do not touch the negative side of these adventurers, which was the capture of natives for slave labor. While part of the Bandeirantes rolled gravel looking for minerals, another wing gave in to the unjust task of arresting and trafficking human beings.

Retake. What happened after the separation of the Iberian crowns?

After 1640, it was no longer known which areas belonged to Madrid and which belonged to Lisbon. In this way, the Spanish government encouraged the Jesuits to restore the Missions of Rio Grande do Sul, which began in 1682. In addition to reactivating San Miguel, they founded the Reductions of San Francisco de Borja (1682), San Nicolas (1682), San Luiz Gonzaga (1687), San Lorenzo Martir (1690), San Juan Bautista (1697) and San Angelo Custodio (1706). These settlements formed the area of the Seven Peoples of the Missions of what is now the southern Brazil. In the territory of the present Paraguay there were eight Reductions, while in Argentina fifteen were founded. By the Treaty of Tordesillas, not only the Colonia del Sacramento (in the south of Uruguay) would have to return to the Spanish crown, but also the whole territory of Rio Grande do Sul would have to be reincorporated. This happened to be the cause of the final conflict in the Guarani Missions.

Organization. How did the administration of the Missions happen?

In each city, the mayor, called *parokaitara* ("the one who decides what to do"), was elected by the residents, but often that choice fell on what already exercised the role of cacique (chief). The Jesuits accepted this situation because they did not want to conflict with the wills and traditions of the tribes. The fact of cultivating and developing the Guarani language, rather than imposing Spanish, was indicative of that purpose. There was also the judge, called *ivirayucu* ("first among those who carry the whip"), responsible for watching over the good customs of the tribe. In order to identify and punish the offenders, he had assistants, who were district court judges, as well as vigilantes, women to care for women, as well as janitors for boys and girls' inspectors. The election of the mayor and other authorities took place on the first day of January of each year and the elect were presented to the priests and then to the governor of the province for confirmation. Each city also counted with accountants, prosecutors, clerks, grocers, and a royal lieutenant.

The buildings were of stone and wood. Beside a large square one had the church, workshops, administrative buildings, cemetery and school, which also served as a residence for the priests. There was also the *coty-guazu* ("communal house"), which housed the widows, the orphans and the unmarried old women. Around the square, the native dwellings were erected, and in the center of it one fastened the statue of the patron saint of the Reduction, near a cross.

Some Guarani customs were at odds with the Christian precepts that the priests intended to see fulfilled. One of those customs was the so-called "extended family", in which monogamous relationships were not clearly enforced. That is why the superior of the Jesuits in the region, the "provincial", issued a provision in 1699 determining that families, consisting of husband and wife, should live in their conjugal residence, without mixing.

The population of the Reductions was in continuous growth,

more by attraction of families of the field than by urban fertility, until in the year 1732 reached the number of 141,242 inhabitants, decreasing since then, counting in 1756, year of the War of the Missions, with 89,536 souls. There was a strong concern of the Jesuits as to the small number of children per couple, so much so that, according to Clovis Lugon, in his "The 'Communist' Christian Republic of the Guaranis", the priests determined, at a determined point, that the sexton vigorously played the bells very early, each day, so that the couple would wake up long enough to have sex before getting ready for work. In the same work it is said that the boys did not directly approach the girls to make the court. The priest was the intermediary of the beginning of the relationship. The young woman told the priest that she intended to date such a young man, and he called the young man to probe his possibilities of acceptance. The choice, as one sees, rested with the woman, but she herself did not expose. If the boy said that he accepted the courtship, the couple would soon be formed. If he refused, the clergyman told the girl that she did not have to suffer any vexation in the community for being rejected, except in front of her confidant, the priest.

Economy. What were the means of life?

In keeping with their centuries-old customs, the catechized Guarani continued to cultivate cassava, potato, corn, mate and cotton, without neglecting the traditions of fishing and hunting, even practicing, with the guidance of clerics, livestock for milk and meat.

The large parcels of land were collectively owned, were called *Tupambaeh* ("God's property" or "God is the owner": *tupan* means "God" and *mbaeh* means "owner"), and vegetables, wheat and cotton were planted in them. In addition to this land system, each head of household could own a small site, the *avambaeh*, of a size that would allow him to plant what was necessary to support his relatives.

There were various types of crafts, with works in gold, silver, iron, wood, leather, cotton and clay, used in the production of containers, clothing, hats, kitchen utensils, furniture, sculptures, paintings and musical instruments, among others. Since trade was encouraged among the various cities, as a form of interaction, each of them specialized in a type of industry.

There was no printed currency, either in banknotes or in metal, so that trade was given in the form of barter, commodity by commodity, certainly following an accounting value, in what today would be understood as virtual currency, or currency of account.

Whether in agriculture, industry, or commerce, the working time was fixed at six hours a day, as it was also in the imaginary Utopia, of Thomas Morus, a work published 93 years before the beginning of the Missions, in the language of the Church, which is Latin. The freedom of action of the Jesuits was ballasted by the purpose of the Spanish crown to give the natives, in terms of rights, the same status as the Iberian individuals.

Religion. How did the priests and the faithful act in the Missions?

After the initial motivation that led to the conquest of America, which was the search for a new passage for India, the greater goal of colonization became the evangelization of the natives, and the Iberian crowns had the order of the Jesuits, a Catholic group formed under military discipline, for doing this doctrinal work.

The bishops in these missions were authorized to ordain the novices as priests, even in adverse conditions outside the traditional seminaries. In the Reductions, priests were not only spiritual, but also secular leaders, being ultimately responsible for economic, social, cultural, and military issues. Generally, there were two priests in each Reduction, one focused on the religious service and the other in charge of temporal and educational matters. The most populous settlements had three fathers.

One of the reasons for the six-hour working time was that there was plenty of time for natives to take part in religious life. Many attended daily masses and, at Sunday Masses and holy days, virtually all of the families were present.

The Province of Paraguay counted on a provincial priest, who directed the thirty Reductions and resided in Cordova, Argentina. The provincial had under his orders the procurators of Santa Fe, Asuncion, and Buenos Aires, and was assisted by two deputy superiors, one who worked in Uruguay and another who was in charge of the Reductions of the Parana basin. Above the provincial there was the general of the Society of Jesus, who resided in Rome and obeyed only the pope.

It should be borne in mind that for the Catholic countries of the seventeenth century, citizenship was synonymous with adherence to Christianity. There was in Europe, before the Enlightenment, no demand for State-religion separation. In the Reductions, the most important task was therefore to baptize and form in the catechism the small natives, in parallel with literacy and basic education.

Education. What attention was paid to school instruction?

That project of Jose Bonifacio de Andrada e Silva, from the early nineteenth century, advocating the installation of a primary school in all the indigenous villages of Brazil, may have been inspired by a decree of the Spanish crown, two centuries earlier. In this, the monarch established that there would be "a school of doctrine and of reading and writing in all places of Indians". If the colonists turned their noses against the decree in most of the Spanish territories, in the thirty towns that made up the Missions the Jesuits tried to implant it in its entirety.

The work of teaching reading, writing and counting in schools involved children from six to twelve years old. Boys and girls studied in separate units and in the curriculum of girls they added the domestic, spinning and cooking arts. Women were thus empowered.

The Jesuit didactic method was based on the manual *Ratio Studiorum*, that had its first edition realized in 1599, by the Roman College. The missionaries translated and published the catechism in the Guarani language, and elaborated a grammar of that language and also a Guarani-Spanish dictionary. They dominated the Guarani and literate the children in their native language, but also taught Spanish. To the children of the leaderships, perhaps intending to gather staff for the Church, they also taught Latin.

From 1700, the Jesuits instituted their own press system, with typographies located in San Javier, Santa Maria la Mayor and Our Lady of Loreto. Many editions published by priests in these graphic offices are still preserved.

Musicality. What was the importance of Music in the Guarani missions?

From the outset the Jesuits were impressed by the ease and the penchant for music among the Guarani. Knowing the sound of European instruments was almost enough to encourage them to manufacture and perform them, as it was the case with the violin, cello and harp.

On the other hand, in school the children sang in choirs. Adults participated in the musical activities of the parish and each city (Reduction) had its choir and its orchestra. The natives not only reproduced the sacred pieces, but also composed, both religious works and secular works. The song Hara Valley Hava (type **bit.ly/2mw0yQd**, numeral "0" in the middle, not the letter "O"), probably from Paraguay, or Bolivia, and Sonata Chiquitana (**bit.ly/2FyvwiG**), this one purely orchestral, of Bolivia, are some examples. They are both anonymous works, but the second, because it shows only European traits, with no trace of American culture, must have been composed by a Jesuit, not by Guarani.

Besides playing instruments and singing with mastery, the Guaranis of the Missions appreciated and cultivated the dance, as their descendants still do today in those lands that did not turn into ruins.

Armies. Did military training exist among the Guarani?

After the incursion by the Bandeirantes in 1641, which imprisoned many Guaranis and forced the Jesuits and the remaining populations to temporarily abandon the Reductions of Rio Grande do Sul, joining the nuclei of Argentina and Paraguay, priests and native leaders saw that it was necessary to organize military detachments to respond to future attacks. In 1652 and 1676 new raids of Bandeirantes invaded the Guarani cities to capture men to be sold as slaves, but in these two occasions the governor of Paraguay repulsed the attacks using its forces, and also, mainly, the military troops formed in the Reductions themselves.

These Guarani detachments were then trained by European militaries, experienced in the Old World wars and coming to South

America called for this purpose, which was to form the armies of the Reductions. As early as the 1652 campaign, the Bandeirantes discovered that the Guarani detachments were equipped with firearms and had shooting training and war tactics that made them fit and competitive in battles.

Not only of Bandeirantes the Guarani of the Missions suffered attacks, but also of tribes that were outside the Jesuit area, like the Guaicurus and the Guarani-Mbyas. These and other tribes were successfully repelled in the several times they attempted invasions.

The Missions armies also helped the Paraguayan government in some war situations in which rebels tried to overthrow the constituted power.

Ruins. In material terms, what is left of the Missions today?

Whenever the Guarani had to face Bandeirantes, adversary tribes or rebels enemies of the provincial government, their military organization showed efficiency. The defeat happened when the enemy became the Portuguese and Spanish crowns in the so-called Guarani War, between 1753 and 1756. The remaining part of those cities lost the relative autonomy they enjoyed, and several Reductions eventually withstand only as ruins. In the twentieth century, Unesco declared seven of the former Reductions as a World Heritage Site.

In 1983, the first of the Reductions to receive the homage it was the site of Sao Miguel das Missoes, in Rio Grande do Sul, Brazil. In 1984 it was the turn of the Argentineans San Ignacio Mini, Our Lady of Santa Ana, Our Lady of Loreto and Santa Maria la Mayor, province of Misiones. Finally, in 1993, Unesco granted the title to two Paraguayan cities, Santissima Trinidad del Parana and Jesus de Tavarangueh, located in Itapua.

7.
The Guarani War

When in 1580 the Portuguese and Spanish crowns were merged as a single empire, after the death in Africa of the young King Dom Sebastiao, without heirs, in 1578, and the death two years later also of his old uncle, the cardinal who was his successor in the royal throne, King Philip II of Spain, grandson of Dom Manuel, the Fortunate, claimed the right to incorporate the Portuguese throne, which was done in what happened to be called "Spanish Dominion", the Treaty of Tordesillas, which had been obsolete in practice, should have been automatically revoked, for it had been signed in 1494 between the crown of Portugal and the crown of Castile, to divide among them the lands both the already discovered ones and those to be discovered, while remaining with Castile the Canary Islands, by the Treaty of Alcacovas, of 1479, and what was to be discovered beyond 370 leagues west of the Island of Santo Antao, in Cape Verde. This constituted a meridian that passed through the present city of Belem, State of Para, and by the present city of Laguna, State of Santa Catarina, Brazil. All the western part of Brazil, with the States of Rio Grande do Sul, Mato Grosso, Amazonas and Amapa, among others, as well as the other western territories, would belong to Castile and, from 1561, to Madrid.

Precedents. How were the decisions of the Iberian crowns seen by the Guarani?

By the papal bull called *Romanus Pontifex*, of 1455, all the discovered lands would belong to Portugal, which began the overseas discoveries in the fifteenth century. The Spaniards soon also threw themselves into the sea and, as we know, it was not Lisbon, but Castile, which financed the voyage of the Genoese Christopher Columbus. The treaty of Alcacovas guaranteed to Portugal the possession of the archipelago of the Azores and the island of Madeira, at the north of the Canary Islands, but also of everything that was to be discovered in the south of these, so that when Columbus arrived in the Bahamas, he was in Portuguese territory.

There was a new conflict between the crowns, which led to the signing of the Treaty of Tordesillas, dividing the world between north and south, but between east and west. As the pope of the time was Spanish, Alexander VI, and had a reputation as corrupt, Portugal demanded that the bilateral agreement, unlike the previous ones, did not carry the papal signature. Only in 1506, with a new Pope, Julius II, the Holy See affixed his signature in the document.

With the return of the division of the crowns, in 1640, Spain proceeded to claim ownership of lands theoretically guaranteed by the treaty, but the situation of the human occupation in the territories diverged frontally from what had been signed. Even before the "Spanish Dominion", the measurement of the 370 leagues was controversial, with navigators arguing that the area of Brazil extended to the region where the Guianas are today.

Finally, in 1750 the *Treaty of Madrid*, or Treaty of Exchange, was signed, referring mainly to that area more coveted by the Portuguese, which was the region of the Missions. Spain wanted the Colonia del Sacramento, which had been taken by the Portuguese in western Uruguay. Portugal imposed as a condition the possession of Rio Grande de Sao Pedro, an area of 500 thousand square kilometers, which included the "Seven People of the Missions", the seven most populated settlements north of the Ibicui River, which were situated San Miguel, San Angelo, San Francisco de Borja, San Juan Bautista, San Lorenzo, San Luiz Gonzaga and San Nicolas, as well as five other smaller settlements. By what was signed, the Colony of the Sacrament returned to Spain, which thus guaranteed the possession of Uruguay, and the Seven Peoples passed to Portuguese Brazil. Guaranis who accepted to be Brazilian would be kept in the territory, while those who preferred the Spanish crown would have to transfer to the south side of the Ibicui River, then in Uruguay, or to the east side of the Uruguay River, in the Argentinean area.

The Guarani judged that anyone staying in Rio Grande de Sao Pedro, now without the protection of the Spanish crown, and without union with the Reductions of the west and the south, would be at the mercy of the Bandeirantes. However, they did not accept to migrate to Uruguay, leaving behind all the cultural and material wealth they have built up over decades.

Bernardo Nusdorffer, superior of the Missions, before the arrival of the news about the Treaty in 1750, ordered that no action was taken until explicit instructions on the procedure to be followed. In April of the following year Buenos Aires received communication from the general of the Society of Jesus, Francisco Retz, ordering that the Treaty of Madrid had to be obeyed. Bernardo Nusdorffer knew the disposition for the resistance among the Guaranis and only in May of 1752 he issued communication to the Reductions giving a year of time for the transfers to be made. As expected, all leaders of the Seven Peoples and the other five smaller settlements in the area refused to comply.

Demarcation. How did the work of demarcating the new borders take place?

Two months later, the Guarani of San Juan Bautista took the weapons depot, which was guarded by the Jesuits. In the same week, the event was repeated in San Miguel and other Reductions. These armies then declared themselves in a state of war. The Jesuits surrendered their positions to the superior, but both he and the governor of Buenos Aires, who then took care of the area, refused to accept the resignation. In September, the commissions in charge of border demarcation arrived with Portuguese and Spanish technicians. The commission of Portugal was headed by Gomes Freire de Andrade, governor of Sao Paulo and Rio de Janeiro, future Count of Bobadela, and the Spanish team was under the orders of Gaspar de Munive, Marquis de Valdelirios, royal commissioner with powers over vice- kings and governors of South America.

In December 1752 the commission set the boundary line on the shores of the Atlantic Ocean and headed north. When it reached the region of San Miguel, in February 1753, in a place today belonging to the municipality of Bage, to install the landmark there, the commission was received not by Jesuits, as planned, but by military detachments of Guarani. The work had to be stopped, the Spaniards going to Montevideo and the Portuguese to Sacramento.

The governor sent Father Luis Altamirano to negotiate, but he returned to Buenos Aires with the same news that had already arrived: the Guarani did not accept the transfer. In parliamentary meeting, they declared that their determination was to remain under the Spanish crown.

At the beginning of 1754, Marquis de Valdelirios returned from Spain, with a royal note ordering the governor of Buenos Aires, Jose de Andonaegui, to take the whole area of the rebel missions to the Portuguese crown.

Battles. Were the Guarani able to confront the Iberian forces?

In an agreement signed with Gomes Freire and Marquis de Valdelirios, the governor set up a 1,500-strong detachment in Rincon de Gallinas, now Rincon de Haedo, at the meeting of the Uruguay River with the Negro River, following from there to the north.

The Portuguese soldiers mounted a fort in Pardo River, but were attacked by the army of the captain Jose Sepee Tiaraju. While warring under bad weather, they succeeded in capturing Tiaraju in April 1754. They kept him in jail, but on the eve of the scheduled execution day he escaped, deceiving the guards.

The bad weather also damaged the advance of the Spanish troops and a column that managed to arrive at the resort of Iapeju was massacred by the army of Chief Rafael Paracatu. The governor then retreated, descending the Ibicui River until again the Uruguay River, but had to confront the Guarani along the way. Later, in the combat of Dayman, he managed to capture Chief Paracatu and take him to Buenos Aires.

One of the results of the conflict was that tribes previously hostile to the Guarani, such as Charruas and Minuans, came to support them. The Portuguese soldiers, seeing that they would not succeed if they continued with that strategy, decided to abandon the struggle, signing the armistice of the Jacui River, in November 1754.

The game turned against the Guarani a year later. Gomes Freire, on the Portuguese side, plus the governor of Buenos Aires, Jose de Andonaegui, and now also the governor of Montevideo, Jose Joaquim de Viana, decided in December 1755 to form a joint army and fight on a single front. Meanwhile, on the Guarani side, the Seven Peoples and small villages also formed a single army under the leadership of Captain Tiaraju.

However, when in early February 1756 the armies of the governors attempted to take San Miguel, the Guarani did not confront them in the open, preferring to resist fighting in guerrilla warfare. In one of these confrontations, occurred in the Mountain of Batovi, the governor of Montevideo killed with his pistol Captain Tiaraju. The Guarani immediately replaced their leader with Chief Nicolas Nanguiru.

The curiosity in this exchange is that Tiaraju was a mythical figure, taken as a kind of saint, by carrying a star-shaped scar on his forehead, understood by the leaders as a kind of predestination. Nanguiru, differently, is a name that means "arrow of the devil".

The Guarani army was finally surrounded at the foot of Cerro Caibateh, on February 10, with the unified troops of the governors having a total of 2,500 men, superiorly equipped, against less than 2,000 Guarani soldiers. In this brutal confrontation, 1,511 Nanguiru soldiers, including the chief himself, were killed and 154 taken prisoner. The rest fled into the forest. Of the Iberian army three Spanish soldiers and one Portuguese died.

With the result of this great battle, the city of San Miguel was captured and the other Reductions surrendered, with the exception of San Lorenzo. A final battle in Chumiebi wiped out what was left of the natives' army, which continued for some time practicing scorched earth policy, setting fire to some of the villages, but the end result was the transfer of the remaining families to the already delimited regions, according to what the Treaty of Madrid had determined in 1750.

Closing. Have the border agreements been fulfilled?

On June 8, 1756, Governor Andonaegui declared in San Miguel that the victory over the Guaranis was assured and the war ended, commencing the transfer of those populations to the western side of the Uruguay River, an Argentine territory.

If the natives were rearranged according to the design of the Spanish and Portuguese crowns, the ownership of the lands was not solved at the end of the tragic Guarani War. The Portuguese were not satisfied with the establishment of the border on the Jacui River, requiring the area to be extended further south. The conflict, however, only came to a solution because of the commitment of two Spanish governors, alongside only one Portuguese governor. The Portuguese felt disadvantaged and did not deliver the Colonia del Sacramento. The Spaniards, in response, did not deliver the area of the Seven Peoples of the Missions.

As for the Jesuits, in 1759 the Portuguese prime minister, Marquis of Pombal, determined their expulsion from the Portuguese dominions. As a direct consequence, education throughout the colony of Brazil was completely disorganized for more than one decade, until, in 1772, state education was officially created, a novelty in the world history, with professors admitted and hired by the public power. (Twenty years later, Condorcet instituted the model in the French Revolution.)

France excluded the Jesuits from their colonies in 1762, while King Carlos III of Spain made an equivalent decision in 1767. To complete these misfortunes of the Jesuits, Pope Clement XIV, by the apostolic brief *Dominius ac Redemptor*, of July 21, 1773, abolished the Society of Jesus, which only after four decades was again authorized by the Holy See, given by Pope Pius VII on August 7, 1814.

Rearrangement. What did the treaty of 1763 say?

After the defeat of the Guarani, Portugal did not have much capacity to support its territorial claims, since it became involved in the Seven Years' War, from 1756 to 1763, forming row with England, against the historical opponent of this, which was France. The two powers, France and England, disputed the possession of Silesia, south of present-day Poland, and also of India and the colonies of North America. France allied with Austria, Russia, Sweden and, from 1761, Spain. To help England, Prussia and Portugal joined, and this coalition got the victory after the long conflict.

In 1761 Charles III of Spain annulled the Treaty of Madrid, replacing it with the *Treaty of El Pardo*. The *Treaty of Paris of 1763* determined that Portugal would maintain the possession of the Colonia del Sacramento and Spain would continue with the area of the Seven Peoples of the Missions. But in 1801, in the War of the

Oranges, the Portuguese retook that territory.

While defeating the caudillo Jose Gervasio Artigas, in the Battle of Taquaremboh, in 1821, the Brazilians annexed the territory of Uruguay, giving it the name *Cisplatina Province*. Artigas had integrated the remnants of the Missions as common citizens with the mestizos and the descendants of Spaniards, but he despised any traces of the natives' own culture.

In 1825, Juan Antonio Lavalleja began a struggle to withdraw Brazilian troops from Uruguay, achieving his intent with the help of the army of Fructuoso Rivera, and on August 25 the Congress of Florida declared Uruguay an independent country. Brazil then declared war on Argentina, beginning a conflict that extended from 1825 to 1828, in what was known as the *War of Brazil and Buenos Aires*, or *Rioplatense War*, between two new countries that were now independent. On August 27, 1828, representatives of Emperor Pedro I of Brazil and the government of the United Provinces of Rio de la Plata signed the *Preliminary Peace Convention*, in which Brazil gave up the Cisplatina Province and agreed to end the war. The frontier was established more to the south, in the Quarai River, and no longer in the Ibicui River.

Possibilities. Was there any chance for independence of the Guarani territory?

While realizing that the Treaty of Madrid used the Reductions as the currency of exchange between the two Iberian crowns, the Guarani came to see as a second great enemy the kingdom of Spain, which for one and a half century acted as protector against the first great enemy, who were the Bandeirantes. Facing Portugal and Spain at the same time, the only prospect for the territory of the Guarani Missions was independence, since the war against the Spanish colonizer would alienate it from the then remote possibility of giving up the delivery of the area to the Portuguese government. And this quitting was what actually occurred after the massacre.

Seeing the "indigenous" individuals as grown children, not as human beings capable of self-determination, prevented the Iberian governments from considering any negotiations aimed at the independence of that territory, which was already very developed by the standards of the time, thanks to the efforts of the Jesuits, who helped the natives to preserve their culture while bringing to them the advances of the European civilization.

The domain and the good performance in the cultivation of arts such as Architecture, Painting, Sculpture, Music, Poetry, Cooking, Ceramics, Luthierie and Clothing, besides the adaptation in the agricultural and artisan professions, gave the Guarani all the necessary structure to manage both the area of the Seven Peoples and that of the entire region of the Missions as an independent, cultured and up-to-date country. In order to train higher level cadres, besides the priests coming from Europe, it would be enough to send a certain number of young people to study in the Iberian universities. In a short time there would be middle and upper-level schools in the main cities of the Missions. But the European governments did not even fear that possibility, because this was not in the horizon of their vision.

Everything would have been different if we had been seen as descendants of peoples of the Far East. If the Europeans had seen us as worthy of respect, we would have been seen as individuals worthy of being invited to the negotiating table.

There would be an only negative point: theocracy. We were still some decades behind the French Revolution, which installed the separation of religion and State, thirty years after the attempt made by Marquis of Pombal in Portugal. The Jesuits, once seen as essential elements in the work of taming the "children" of the new world, came to be seen as an evil to be extirpated after the Guarani War. If the protected natives were rebelled as if they were adults, the Europeans saw no other explanation than the form of education that the priests ministered, leading the Guarani to believe that they could be equal to the colonizers, in law, in military power and in political power.

Independence. Did the Guarani War instigate Argentine independence?

The Jesuits were in disgrace, with a forbidden religious activity, until the restoration decreed by Pius VII, four months after

Napoleon was deposed in France and in the midst of the return negotiations of the Bourbon monarchy, in the person of Louis XVIII. The anticlerical Masonic power begun with Marquis of Pombal in Lisbon, in 1755, seemed to be closed now, with the fall of Napoleon, in 1814. Under this view, the Holy See authorized the return of the Society of Jesus, but the world was very different now, with some independent countries in the Americas and with spaces now much restricted for action of the Jesuits.

Yes, the cost of the Guarani War for the Iberian crowns was much higher than the casualties and material expenses. The armies of Montevideo and Buenos Aires, as well as that of Gomes Freire, were formed by a large proportion of settlers born in the New World. In the battles against the natives, as had also occurred in North America, these soldiers discovered that they had stuff to confront the European rulers. They and the natives were children of the same land, though with some difference of blood. Decimating sibling children from the same piece of ground to secure the power of European kings did not seem like a very sensible business.

The children of the United States rebelled in 1775, making their declaration of independence against England the following year. In 1810, 35 years later, it was the turn of the Platense armies to rebel against the Spanish crown, obtaining the independence of the United Provinces of the Rio de la Plata, which happened to be Argentina.

Eschatology. What is the "land without evils"?
The divine promise of the Terrestrial Paradise has been part of the Guarani tradition since millennial times. After the contact with the Christian theology, some adaptation was made to this native belief, so that today it is difficult to know what is original and what is a mixture. This is the myth of the *Ivy Maran ei* ("land without evils"), in which the natives can enter into life, without first having to die and be resurrected.

There, the crops grow and thrive without anyone having to plow the land and sow. Cassava flour, *mbeiu* (or beiju, a pankake of cassava), meats, honey and other foods appear already ready to be eaten. There is no death, no pain no sorrow.

Some shamans claimed to have seen in their dream the exact

location of this land, and urged the families to go out in search of it. Crossing rivers and waterfalls through the hinterland, fighting against hostile tribes and contracting diseases, many indigenous groups left to return, having achieved nothing like what had been promised to them. Many say that it is necessary to walk to the east, others, to the west, and there is no consensus on this point.

As the myth also reached the Tupi tribes, they say that a group of 12,000 natives left the northeast coast of Brazil in search of this land, in 1539, arriving in Peru years later only with a group of 300 people, who were the ones that remained alive

The interference of the biblical account may have influenced the explanation that follows about the emergence of this place. One day Nanderu ("our father"), who corresponds to Yahweh, decided to destroy mankind, because of the iniquity that has been spread through every corner. But there was a just man, whom the Creator decided to preserve. This man was Guiraypoty ("Bird River Shrimp"), who corresponds to Noah. Nanderu directed him to build a house using taquara (a thin kind of bamboo) and other light materials. When the great flood came the house of Guiraypoty floated and he, always inside it, sailed for days until arriving at the land without evils. He is the messenger who brought the news of the existence of this place and also the promise of the Creator that one day people will live there, without war, famine, disease, aging, ignorance, depression, crimes or prisons.

8.

Battles in the North

There remain 135 native languages in the United States, which are spoken by little more than 370,000 inhabitants. Many of these languages today have very few speakers and are about to disappear, since young people practice English and express themselves with difficulty in the language of their ancestors.

In 1975 the country approved the Indian Self-Determination and Education Assistance Law, which guaranteed the establishment of autonomous governments in the reservations, responding directly to the federal government.

These governments of the native peoples, like the state governments, have no right to declare war, to establish independent relations with foreign governments, or to mint or print money. The total number of officially recognized tribal governments is 562, spread over several reservations in several states of the federation.

Unlike the South American natives, who for the most part lived in hollows, which were houses made of wood and straw, the northern Amerindians, when Europeans arrived, were sheltering in sharp tents made of animal skins.

Colonization. Did British have a good welcome in Virginia?

British came to America in the early seventeenth century, long after the Iberians, who had arrived at the end of the fifteenth century. In 1607 the first English families established settlements in Tsenacommacah, current State of Virginia, with the consent of the natives of the region, the Powhatan people, led by Chief Wahunsunacock, who was the father of Pocahontas.

This native girl, born in 1595, had a role similar to that practiced a few decades before in Sao Paulo by Bartira, the daughter of Chief Tibiriça, who married a European and had several descendants. Pocahontas, who was also called Matoaka, grew up playing with the settlers' sons and had good traffic between the two peoples, natives and immigrants. In 1608 Powhatans warriors imprisoned the leader of the colony, Captain John Smith, and settlers asked her to intercede in favor of the European. She did it, and saved the captain's life. Sometime later, one of the settlers, John Rolfe, went on to date her. He asked the then Governor Sir Thomas Dale to marry her, and he was served. Baptized, she was given the Christian name of Rebecca. Taken to meet England, and speak to the royal couple, there she contracted smallpox and died.

The language spoken by the tribe was the Algonquian and the population in the year of the arrival of the Europeans, 1607, was about 20 thousand people, spread over 30 tribes, of which there are today about four thousand individuals. They occupied not only the east of Virginia, but also part of the present State of Maryland. Each of these tribes had its leader, but all paid tribute to the Powhatan chief, who was Wahunsunacock, maintaining a federative State developed in the late sixteenth century.

With the death of Wahunsunacock, in 1618, his brother Opchanacanough went on to rule the Powhatan nation. Unlike the older brother, the new chief was hostile to the British settlers and initiated negotiations for them to leave the region. One of the reasons is that many natives had died, mainly children, who were infected by contagious diseases brought by Europeans, such as rubella and measles, and against which they had no immunity. In the view of the natives, something very wrong these new inhabitants were bringing, once the natives' children died and the settlers survived. This same motivation must have led Pikeroby to his warlike actions a century earlier in Sao Paulo.

The new Powhatan chief made two strong attacks on the Europeans, one in 1622, another in 1644, but colonists with better armaments and ammunition took advantage. The result was that in this second clash the English decimated the Powhatan nation, almost leading it to extinction.

In 1620, two years before the first attack of the Powhatan chief in Virginia, it was the turn of the British to set up their colony on the coast of Massachusetts, founding the settlement that would later become the city of Plymouth. The Europeans who settled there needed to expand their area of action, with new lands for agriculture, hunting and extractivism. Thus, in 1625 they presented their intention to occupy an area in Pemaquid, of about 5,000 hectares. The natives of the Abenaki tribe, also of the Algonquian linguistic branch, saw those lands as "property of the Great Spirit", but Chief Samoset yielded to the settlers' pretense as a policy of good neighborliness and signed the agreement by drawing a sign on a sheet of paper that the English brought him. This year, 1625, marks the first official assignment of native lands to British settlers in North America.

The situation of Europeans was much more complicated in New Holland, now New York. The governor-general of the colony, the Dutchman Willem Kieft, sent in 1643 a military detachment to punish the Mohicans for their non-collaborative attitude. Certainly Kieft was aware of Plymouth's happy agreement between the English and the Abenakis. In this Dutch attack four Mohicans were killed. In response, the natives killed four settler soldiers. The Dutch then set up a total war plan. While surprising the native villages at dawn, the soldiers invaded the tents and indiscriminately killed men, women, and children by bayonet blows. The hostilities extended until 1645, being seen exterminated then the nation of the Mohicans.

These genocidal actions of the governor had a bad reception at court, which replaced him in 1647 by Peter Stuyvesant. Back in Europe to stand trial, Kieft died in a wreck on September 27 of the same year, off the coast of Wales.

Phillip. What action of English against natives revolted Chief Phillip?

By 1619 another federation of tribes, the Wampanoag, who lived south of Massachusetts and east of Rhode Island, suffered an epidemic of smallpox that nearly wiped out the entire population. Some current scholars believe that the disease was more characteristic of leptospirosis than of smallpox. By cultivating corn and beans, they formed a people in good financial condition by the standards of the time. But that mortality made room for the English to occupy lands in these areas formerly occupied by the many thousands of natives.

Chief Massasoit had great friendship with the Mayflower pilgrims, so that his second son, Metacom, adopted a biblical codename, which he learned from the English: Phillip. When Phillip succeeded his older brother in 1662, he began a period of hostilities in front of the settlers. In 1671 the settlers forced their men to surrender their firearms and forced him to sign a peace treaty. In 1675 some of his men assassinated a native allied to the colony of Plymouth, and, by punishment, the English there hanged three Wampanoags. Phillip, then known as King Phillip, sewed an alliance with Chief Narragansett, adding vast number of tribes, to attack the English colonies.

Throughout the conflict, almost all settlements of the natives were destroyed. King Phillip then fled to Mount Hope, but was caught and killed by settler soldiers, as they did his ally Narragansett too. Even with the death of the chief, Englishmen and natives continued the war, which was only closed with the Treaty of Casco Bay in 1678. The so-called *King Phillip's War* is regarded by historians as the most devastating clash between English colonists and natives of the United States during colonial times.

March. At what stage of History did the occupation of the "American Old West" motivate conflicts with the natives?

The next major conflicts between natives and settlers occurred after the independence of the thirteen eastern colonies and the territorial expansion phase known as the occupation of the "American Old West".

After independence in 1776, former British settlers, now Yankee citizens, officially "*US Americans*", began their expansion westward without facing many significant resistance from either the Spaniards or the natives, since there was a very vast territory, before a small contingent of Iberian colonists to occupy it. As for the French possessions, the Seven Years' War resulted in a victory for the British, aided by the Portuguese, so that by the *Treaty of Paris of 1763* the lands formerly occupied by France in North America were declared British possessions. By a later agreement, the population of Quebec, Canada, was granted the right to maintain French language and customs, provided they continued to accept English rule, a situation that persists at the beginning of the twenty-first century.

Also Louisiana, part of New France in the southern United

States, became an English colony from 1763, and persisted practicing the French language parallel to English until at the beginning of the twentieth century a determination of the federal government banned primary education French-speaking, making the state's educated youth speak exclusively English. In the year 1800, Napoleon Bonaparte pressured Spain to return to France the Louisiana colony, which only re-belonged to the United States in 1803, by means of indemnification of 15 million dollars.

The great conflicts with natives by force of the occupation of the West began during the *Anglo-American War*, of 1812, when the English tried to return to the territory of the United States like colony.

Tecumseh. What advantage did Chief Tecumseh envisage when he ally himself with the English in 1812?

The natives saw an opportunity to avenge the incursions of the Yankees, and, forming a confederation encompassing the west and south, allied themselves with the English, hoping that they would return to administer the colonies of the east, leaving the old west in its peace. Something not very well remembered in the United States is that the new capital, Washington, at the age of 14, was burned down and destroyed in this war, which is also called the *Tecumseh War*.

Chief Tecumseh ("Fugazing Star"), born in 1768, in Ohio, at the age of 21 became the leader of the Shawnee people. In 1808 he expanded his area of influence, building the great Confederation of Tecumseh, uniting tribes of various ethnicities and languages. That year, he founded, along with his brother Tenskwatawa, nicknamed "the Prophet", in the place where today is Lafayette, Indiana, the indigenous town of Prophetstown, which became the capital of what should be, according to his expectative, a large native State, covering territories of the southern United States, the northwest and the east of the Mississippi River, with the support of the British, who already saw advantage in the alliance. It was in this way that the British, with the western rearguard of the confederate nations, under the command of Tecumseh, and also the involvement of several provinces of Canada, issued on June 18, 1812, against the United States of America the attack that sought to re-conquer the colonies.

The war lasted until February 18, 1815, although the Treaty of Ghent, declaring peace, was signed on December 24, 1814.

There were, at the beginning of 1812, two types of division among the United States authorities. On the one hand, many came to admire the French Revolution, forming the group of Republicans, who wanted a unitary State, like that of France. On the other hand, the group of Federalists, who worked for the strengthening of the member states, were consolidated. The other division was even more worrisome: Southern states continued to market products with the British, following the blockade by the British government in retaliation for Napoleon Bonaparte's expansionist policy.

The English, through the provinces of Canada and their alliance with the Confederation of Tecumseh, attempted to force the northern states to abandon trade with France and re-open space for British business.

Given the news that British ships were imprisoning American ships on the high sea, President James Madison asked Congress to authorize the war. The Federalists offered resistance at first, but the result of the vote was favorable to the presidential proposal.

Facing at the same time the British coming from Canada, the British navy arriving by the sea and the army of the Tecumseh natives from Michigan, the United States forces encountered difficulties beyond what was anticipated to keep ahead. Otherwise, Canada could most probably have been incorporated, or won a pledge to declare full independence against the British crown.

Already in the beginning of the conflict, the army of Tecumseh and the British forces took Fort Detroit. The United States navy, in reprisal, seized control of Lake Erie in 1813, forcing the British-Indian alliance to withdraw to Canada. Soon the alliance was attacked there by the United States, and at the *Battle of the Thames*, Tecumseh was killed on October 5 of that year.

Without Tecumseh, the situation seemed more favorable to US troops in early 2014. However, after Napoleon's fall in April and his confinement on Elba Island, the British felt more strengthened to intensify their confrontation with the former colonies. Towards the end of the year, an army of 4,000 men was landed in Benedictine.

Soldiers who tried to prevent the advance of these troops were defeated in Bladensburg. With this the English dominated Washington-DC, setting fire to the White House, the Library of Congress, and many other public buildings, as well as private homes.

After peace was established, with the recognition of the absence of victory for the British and Americans, the United States rebuilt the capital, improving the architecture of public buildings, starting with the White House, and nourishing national pride more strongly.

The Confederation of Tecumseh was dismantled and the tribes that participated of it were moved to regions more to the west, leaving the east of the Mississippi. Land occupations of natives have been intensified by Yankee farmers ever since. Tecumseh remains venerated as a hero by the natives of both the United States and Canada.

Jackson. Where did the battle that turned Jackson a national hero occur?

The most prominent general in the Tecumseh War, though he did not directly confront that chief, for geographical reasons, was Andrew Jackson, who in 1829 became the seventh president of the United States, re-elected in 1832 for a second four-year term, until 1837.

In 1813, influenced by the Confederation of Tecumseh, the Creek natives, of Alabama, created a federation, joining to the Red Stick tribe. Responding to the expansion of farmers, they started the *Creek War*, which, like the Tecumseh War, received English support. The Red Stick tribe also helped Admiral Cochrane advance over New Orleans. With the defeat of Cochrane, the conflict was ended with the *Treaty of Fort Jackson*, of August 1814, in which General Andrew Jackson forced Federation Creek to deliver him an area of more than 8.5 million hectares of land, covering Alabama and southern Georgia. With the victory over the English in New Orleans, Jackson became a national hero, which gave him a seat to become president. In recognition of his bravery, the National Congress gave him a gold medal in February 1815.

Between 1816 and 1818 Jackson undertook a highly effective military campaign to take Florida from Spain. The strategy consisted in defeating the Seminole tribe, which maintained control of the area. At different stages and locations, Crocktown, Chickasaw, and Cherokee tribesmen also fell victim to Jackson.

A Tennessee-born lawyer, General Andrew Jackson, nicknamed Old Hickory, was the first president born out of the original thirteen colonies, and was also the first president of the Democratic Party, once, in his term, Republicans were divided into Republican Democrats, his line, and National Republicans, opposed to him. Authoritarian and demagogic, he tried to abolish the electoral college and had little appreciation for the decisions of the National Congress, using his veto power with unusual frequency.

It was during his term, under a law of 1830, that these tribes he defeated were confined to a reservation west of the Mississippi River. But the following year, 1831, a man from the Sioux Hunkpapa tribe destined to make history in the struggle for resistance to the occupation of land by the Euro-descendants would be born in South Dakota: Sitting Bull.

In 1834, still under the Jackson administration, Congress passed the "Trade Regulation, Indigenous Tribes Relation and Peacekeeping at Borders Act". This legislation determined that the territory between western Mississippi and the States of Missouri, Louisiana, and Arkansas was indigenous property, barred from entering any white without the express authorization of the Army. Settlers had already moved west and created the States of Iowa and Wisconsin, prompting the government to re-mark the boundaries of the indigenous territory from the Mississippi River to 95° Meridian. Several Army posts were erected along the Mississippi, Missouri, Arkansas and Red Rivers, in addition to Fort Jesup, Louisiana.

During his presidency, Jackson visited one of the great native warriors, Black Hawk, born in Illinois, in the Sahu tribe, who did not become chief but who led battles in the Anglo-American War, allied with the English. He lived from 1767 to 1838 and, by refusing to move his tribe from the Mississippi, undertook in 1932 the *Black Hawk War* against the United States Army, when he was defeated and imprisoned after months of conflict, even though he was aided by the Fox, Winnebago and Kickapoo tribes. He later wrote his autobiography, which he launched in 1833. After receiving the presidential visit, he was persuaded to make trips through the interior of the country, in army boats, with the aim of trying to convince natives of the various regions to avoid colliding with the United States, since these struggles had no other outcome but defeat, no matter how long they lasted.

In the meantime, in 1835, four miners secretly entered the sacred mountains of the Lakota tribe, or Sioux Teton Lakota, in search of gold. As soon as they were discovered by the natives, a detachment of warriors attacked them, leaving a balance of three dead. The one who escaped wrote on a sheet of paper: "All were killed but me". These miners were unsuccessful in their endeavor, but were the pioneers of the Gold Rush in the Black Hills area of South Dakota.

Gold. In what year did the "Gold Rush" culminate?

Andrew Jackson ended his passage through the White House in 1837, but he did not see any decline of his influence on the United States course. In addition to electing his successor, Martin Van Buren, he continued to formulate national policies, such as the proposal of annexation of the Republic of Texas, which happened to take place in 1845, by choice of Texans, independent of Mexico since 1836. His design of confinement of natives, in territories protected by the Army, which did not disturb the conquest of the west, was consolidated as a national consensus among the descendants of Britons and also of Dutch, as it was the case of Van Buren, a son of merchants of the State of New York. Already in the second year of this new president's term, the eighth in the country, in 1838, the beginning of gold exploration in the Cherokee lands of Oklahoma led to the confinement of this tribe, under the watchful eye of General Winfield Scott.

The opening of the Oregon Trail in 1842, through native territories, ushered in a new phase of expansion, which peaked in January 1848, in the California "Gold Rush" explosion.

A month later, February 1848, the *Treaty of Guadalupe Hidalgo* was signed, which ended the war between Mexico and the United States, with the first transferring to the latter, in the so-called Mexican Cession, large portions of what happened to be known as the

American Old West.

Following the discreet Gold Rush in Georgia, begun in 1829, it was the turn of the discovery of the ore at Sutter's Mill, Sierra Nevada, Coloma district, El Dorado, California, by the explorer James W. Marshall. This time it was not only the inhabitants of the United States, but also of many other countries, that arrived in great caravans, after crossing indigenous territories. The number of these new inhabitants is estimated at 300,000, collecting miners and their families along with other adventurers in search of business with those who, fortunate, prospected some nugget.

Those who came ashore, from the east and also from the Oregon, faced resistance from the natives, but the perspective of enriching with the gold prospecting led them to promote killings and expulsions and move on towards El Dorado. These became known as the "forty-niners", in reference to the year in which the largest flow occurred, which lasted until 1855.

About half of that contingent arrived in California by sea, which included Latin Americans, Hawaiians, and even Chinese. Already in the year 1850 California became a state, the 31st of the Union, without going through the federal territory phase.

Most of these prospectors were imbued with the belief in the *Manifest Destiny*, a doctrine launched in a Washington-DC newspaper editorial by publisher John Louis O'Sullivan, in 1845, as a basis of support for the annexation proposal of Texas and Oregon, with probable authorship of the columnist Jane Cazneau, and that preached that the United States had the mission to civilize the continent, by divine determination, redeeming the west and giving example to the Old World. O'Sullivan, son of diplomats, was later ambassador to Portugal ("US Minister to Portugal"), between 1853 and 1857. In the years of the gold fever, and for two more decades, the Democratic Party embraced the cause preached by him, although in the Republican Party several important names have rejected it, as it was the case of Abraham Lincoln and Ulysses S. Grant. Many believe that the idea of "American exceptionalism" is a byproduct of the doctrine of Manifest Destiny.

As a result of the numerous conflicts between natives and

pioneers heading west, the US government signed the *Fort Laramie Treaty* in September 1851, with representatives of the Sioux, Cheyenne, Arapaho, Crow, Mandan, Hidatsa and Arikara, on the banks of the Laramie River, Wyoming, determining the demarcation of indigenous territories that would be free of encroachment or occupation of settlers, with a guarantee of passages such as that of the Oregon Trail and permission for the construction of highways that the government considered necessary, where Yankee citizens would pass without risk of attacks by natives. A second Fort Laramie Treaty was signed after the Civil War, in 1868, with the Sioux, Arapaho, Lakota, and others, and the government undertook to provide incentives for agriculture, English language education and also the allocation within the reservations of Euro-descendant professionals, such as teachers, blacksmiths, farmers, engineers, millers and federal employees. It was also guaranteed in this second treaty the possession of the sacred area of the Black Mountains to the Lakota tribe.

Pre-war. How was the Navajo tribe on the eve of the Civil War?

In November 1860 Abraham Lincoln was elected president and the following month, on December 20, the State of South Carolina declared itself separated from the Union, giving the first signal to the Civil War (1861-1865). By that time the government saw the conflicts with some tribes as solved problems, calling the Cherokees, Choclaws, Creeks, Chickasaws and Seminoles the "Five Civilized Tribes". But the Sioux, the largest indigenous nation in the country, and many other native peoples were far from achieving peace with the pioneers and the government.

The *Sioux Santee* tribe, led by Little Crow, had its base in the State of Minnesota, which in 1858 extended its borders more than 100 kilometers to the west. Little Crow had decided that he would not sign any further cession of territory, but it was clear that his men had no power to meet federal troops if there was a confrontation. In the midst of the desolation that the natives lived in, the Congress passed in 1860 the law called the "Pre-Emption Bill", declaring "free lands" in the west many territories occupied by Indians and coveted by settlers.

The Teton *Oglala Sioux* tribe, or Lakota, was led by Red Cloud, who after the Civil War fought a series of fierce fights with federal troops. The Hunkpapa branch also belonged to the Teton Sioux nation, and it came to make history for its bravery in the defense of native lands.

The *Sioux Nakota* tribe, or Yankton Sioux, which has the Assiniboine group as the best known, cousins of the Stoney group of Canada, considered its land problems resolved after the signing of the first Fort Laramie Treaty. The situation differed greatly from that of the other two large Sioux branches, the Santee and the Teton. Also the Cheyenne tribe, that in its northern fraction divided territories with the Sioux nation, looked for alliance with the Teton Sioux tribe to face the invaders of its lands. The southern branch of the Cheyenne tribe of the River Platte relied on the preparation of its young heads, Hook Nose and Tall Bull.

In the southern plains the Comanches were scattered in many small communities, but had as big warrior chief the leader Ten Bears, besides consecrating an alliance with the Kiowa tribe, which had among its warlords Lone Wolf, Satanta ("White Bear"), and Kicking Bird.

The Apaches Chiricahua counted, from 1858, with the leadership of the chief nicknamed by the Mexicans as Geronimo, who fought both against Mexican troops and against United States troops.

The Navajo tribe, led by Manuelito, had been acculturated by the Spaniards and now lived in agriculture and livestock, without presenting any concern to the United States government. Meanwhile, the Ute tribe had been not only pacified, but also transformed into an ally of the government.

Secession. What support did the confederates expect in the conflict?

Even under the vertiginous effects of the Gold Rush, which stressed conflicts with numerous native tribes, it was not these struggles that led the United States to wage the greatest wars of the American continent in their entire history. The war of the Secession

Crisis, begun on April 12, 1861, when Confederate troops seized Fort Sumter, South Carolina, was motivated by the decision to maintain black slavery by a group of southern states.

Elected, President Lincoln had made clear his purpose of preventing the advance of slavery in the United States, according to the Republican Party's electoral platform. The states of the southern, more agrarian region, soon began to rebel against this prospect and decided to create the Confederate States of America, initially with seven states, on March 4, 1861, before the inauguration of the new president. James Buchanan, Democrat, still in office, declared illegal the formation of the confederation, which months later instituted the city of Richmond, Virginia, as its capital. Washington-DC, then a 61-year-old artificial city, 47 years post-rebuilding after being destroyed by the British, was not yet a consolidated capital with historical status, since it requires more than a century.

The gold standard, begun in 1789 as gold-silver bimetalism and consolidated in gold in 1850 by the scarcity of silver, served to prevent the inflation of the new capital, but it did not prevent costly, high interest rates and credit restrictions. However, the possibility of the end of the slave labor force was the visible tip of the economic problem in the understanding of those who wanted to maintain the system.

Lincoln said he would not agree to start any war, but the capture of Fort Sumter led him to summon US troops to resume the site. The Union resumed the fort, but as the fighting unfolded, it added four more southern states: Virginia, Arkansas, Tenessee and North Carolina. These joined the initial rebels South Carolina, Mississippi, Florida, Alabama, Georgia, Louisiana and Texas. They were allied as southern states, but, geographically, they are located in the southeast of the country. In the north and west, at that time, slavery was already banned in several states, and free blacks participated in the war against the South for both the purposes of the Union and the humanitarian interest in liberating siblings descendants of people from sub-Saharan Africa.

The Confederates strengthened under the belief that the Europeans would intervene in their favor, since those ones needed the cotton they produced. However, during the four years of conflict this support never occurred.

Near the end of 1862 the Confederates were defeated at the *Battle of Antietam*, in Maryland, and this led Lincoln to edit the *Emancipation Proclamation*, according to which the end of the war, if the Union were victorious, would have to result in the abolition of slavery.

Comprising the Union, and battling against the eleven Confederate States, 22 states and seven territories, located to the north and west, were together. The fight was clearly uneven and Richmond's defeat to Washington-DC was only a matter of time. After the Battle of Antietam, the Confederates might have realized that their chances were small, surrendering to the stronger side. But the increase from seven to eleven states before the end of that episode gave them hope that they would continue to expand, which did not happen either. And the fight continued for three more years, until May 9, 1865, with a balance of more than 800 thousand dead. The surrender of General Robert E. Lee from the Confederate army to General Ulysses S. Grant, commander of Union troops, however, occurred a month earlier, on April 9, at the *Battle of Appomattox Court House*.

Four years of struggle happened, in which the Union, counting on the more developed northern states, destroyed, inch by inch, the navy and the armies of the Confederates, leaving at the end of the conflict a group of eleven states devastated in their economies and infrastructures, that needed to be rebuilt. At the end of the year 1865 the Congress approved the 13th amendment to the Constitution, abolishing slavery completely in the country. The Union occupied and guarded the Confederate States until 1877, and in that period, it employed several black people in positions of command. This attitude of the government stirred up the mood and motivated the creation of secret societies against the blacks, as it was the case of the Ku Klux Klan.

Participation. How many American Indians are estimated to have participated in the Civil War?

The natives were not alien to the scene of the civil war. Most

Cherokee tribes, for example, fought alongside the Union at the outset of the conflict, switching sides soon after, in a miscalculation motivated by previous feuds with the federal government, but also by having the Civil War overtaken these natives in internal warfare, among its own members.

Rebel leader Stand Watie was facing Chief John Ross at the beginning of the conflict. In a short time he aligned himself with the Confederates, obtaining the rank of colonel. John Ross wanted to remain neutral, but he also gave in to the Confederates, agreeing to transfer to them the obligations of the treaty signed with the Union, receiving confederate protection, as well as aid in cattle, tools and other goods. In mid-1862 the Union Army captured John Ross, keeping him imprisoned until the end of the war. Defeated, he declared loyalty to the Union troops.

Some other tribes were also divided, with some branches fighting alongside the Confederates and others alongside the Union.

In addition to the Cherokees, among the native nations involved in the war we can remember Creeks, Seminoles, Delawares, Pequots, Powhatans, Iroquois, Chickasaws, Ojibwes, Choctaws, Lumbees, Senecas, Catawbas, Potawatomis, Oneidas, Hurons, Mohawks, Odawas, Osages and Kickapoos.

In total, an estimated number of 25,000 indigenous people participated in the Civil War.

At least two major fights had indigenous territory as their stage.

The first of these was the *Battle of Cabin Creek*, on the banks of the Rio Grande, in Oklahoma, in July 1863. The second and last major confrontation within the Indian area occurred near the first one, in September 1864, and ended in victory for the Confederate side.

The Lumbee, Pamunkey, Iroquois, and Powhatan tribes, scattering themselves throughout the states of Virginia, North Carolina, and Pennsylvania, helped Union troops in various ways. The Lumbees, for example, acted in guerrilla warfare, while the Pamunkeys worked as pilots of the naval force. The Powhatans served as river pilots, forest guides and spies.

General Ely S. Parker, a native of the Seneca tribe, drafted the terms of the surrender that General Ulysses S. Grant presented to

General Robert E. Lee. Grant's secretary in the final months of the conflict, at first Parker had difficulty in seeing his value as a military being recognized, because he was not a Euro-descendant. But war, although it is said that it brings the first victim to the truth, in this case had the merit of joining blacks, natives and whites in a common struggle, at least among the forces of the Union. In the military as well as in the world of exact sciences, pragmatism tends to prevail over provincial and ethnic prejudices, which weakened both the Confederate army in the nineteenth century and the Nazi army in the twentieth century.

When Robert E. Lee, defeated, said he was happy to see a true American there, Parker replied: "We are all Americans". This is an indigenous vision: we are all children of the American continent. The Euro-descendants and Afro-descendants were well received, and if there were wars, this was for lack of understanding and for greed, because there was land for all.

Contrary. Why did the Chickasaws allied with the Confederates?

Not only did the Cherokees evaluate that they would have an advantage in supporting the Confederates. There were farmers among members of the Creek and Choctaw nations who were slave owners. Many of them did not want to lose their manpower, which reached almost 6,000 servants, and saw a gain in allying themselves to the confederate states, hoping to reject the tendency to abolish slavery. Also among the Chickasaws, Seminoles and Catawbas occurred this division, with part of the native branches fighting alongside the southern armies.

The Choctaws were also divided and those who aligned themselves with the Confederates fought initially with ardor. Jackson McCurtain, one of the chiefs of that nation, served as lieutenant colonel for the First Choctow Battalion in Oklahoma. Little by little, however, the enthusiasm of the Choctaws was being emptied, when they realized that the Confederate command did not help them financially, leaving them without tents, clothes and supplies.

For the Chickasaws, the motive for alignment to the South was the measure of land transfer, when the federal government took them to areas that were already occupied by other tribes and this has caused conflicts. As the Union did not give them protection against the enemy tribes, they made bet in the adhesion to the army of the confederates.

Chiefs. After the Civil War, did Indians continue still under attack?

After the Civil War, the victorious side, the Union, was busy rebuilding the area of the eleven states of the Southeast that had struggled to maintain the servile condition of the black population. The native tribes seemed safer at the time, but it was not long before new attacks on indigenous territories restored the era of confrontation between Euro-descendants and "red skins". Several generals who excelled in the Civil War later used their tactics in fighting Indian armies, as it was the case of Phillip Henry Sheridan, author of the phrase "Good Indian is Dead Indian", and the most famous of all, George Armstrong Custer.

Sitting Bull. Amongst all the chiefs who fought battles against settlers or military detachments of the federal government, the most notable was the leader of the Sioux Teton Hunkpapa tribe, Sitting Bull, who lived between 1831 and 1890.

In 1876, Sitting Bull formed an army of 3,500 men, joining Sioux branches and Cheyenne allies, and faced the Seventh American Cavalry Regiment, led by General Custer. At the *Battle of Little Bighorn*, on June 25, he inflicted heavy defeat on that detachment. Custer, then 36, already very famous for his role in the Civil War and for his attacks on the natives, was killed there, along with his two brothers.

The United States Army then used every effort available on a hunt for the Sioux chief. Sitting Bull and his men took refuge in Canada, where they tried to establish residence. Queen Victoria, however, did not agree to grant land to a native army pursued by the United States, fearing that the Sitting Bull presence there would instigate the local natives to confront the subjects of the British crown. In 1881 he decided to return and present himself to the federal forces of the United States in an act of surrender.

Having defeated General Custer, a legend of the Civil War, who obtained his rank of brigadier general at the age of only 23, and was later given a commendation for bravery, he himself, Sitting Bull, for this feat also became a legend. He is considered one of the most important military leaders in world history.

Withdrawn from the wars, he became part of Buffalo Bill's traveling theater, with whom he traveled through innumerable cities in the interior of the country.

Years later, he became embroiled in the mystical leader Wovoca, of the Paiute tribe, who called himself the new Jesus Christ and had developed a ritual called "Ghost Dance". Wovoca convinced Sitting Bull that, with his dance, the natives could make the ground open and swallow all the descendants of Old World immigrants, leaving the land again in the hands of the natives.

The adherence of Sitting Bull to that sect, attracting with his notoriety an increasing number of natives, caused that the federal government happened to see in the movement a great threat. He sent an indigenous police station to arrest him. He resisted arrest and, together with his son, was shot and killed.

Sitting Bull and his friend Buffalo Bill

Geronimo. After Sitting Bull and Tecumseh, the most notable chief among the natives of North America is the Apache Geronimo, who was born in 1829 and died in 1909.

From early he gained renown in his tribe as an exceptional hunter. From the first hunt he killed, as a teenager, he ate the raw heart, to ensure that in all his future hunts he would be successful. By the age of seventeen he had already led incursions into the territory of several enemy tribes.

Years later, an invasion of Mexican soldiers in his tribe killed his wife, his mother and his children. At one of his retreats in the forest he heard voices. They told them that he would not be shot in battle and that a power from on high would guide his footsteps when he sought revenge against the Mexicans who murdered his family.

For over ten years Geronimo and his men chased and killed Mexicans. The ensuing war between Mexico and the United States brought new configuration to the jurisdiction over the lands and this generated a new kind of enemy for the tribe. Geronimo's stepfather, Cochise, signed an agreement with the United States government guaranteeing protection over the Apache territory. But after Cochise's death, colonists and soldiers began to disrespect both that agreement and the leadership of Geronimo, promoting invasions on their lands.

After years of fighting between the Geronimo Apaches and US federal government soldiers, the natives surrendered. Geronimo and his warriors were arrested, ending in those days the life of this remarkable man's struggles.

Red Cloud. Chief Red Cloud, of the Sioux Lakota tribe, had a longer life than the Apache leader Geronimo, for he was born earlier, in 1922, and died in 1919, the same year as the Apache.

In what is now the State of Nebraska, he grew up seeing wars between his tribe and the neighboring Crow and Pawnee tribes. In 1841, therefore at the age of 19, he killed a rival of the chief who created him and who was his uncle. With the act he divided the tribe, but raised respect.

The territory of his tribe was rich in gold, which attracted adventurers and military from 1862. Thus, between 1866 and 1868, Red Cloud fought several battles against government detachments, obtaining gains in these struggles of resistance and causing the government to sign the Treaty of Fort Laramie, which guaranteed natives the right to various portions of land in Nebraska, South Dakota, Wyoming, and Montana.

In 1874, however, new invasions broke the commitment expressed in that Treaty, and the dreaded "Red Cloud Wars" began again. However, knowing the advantages of peaceful life, the chief sought talks with government representatives, always trying to preserve the guarantees previously earned.

Little Crow. Years before those of Red Cloud's acting, Chief Little Crow, of the Sioux Dakota tribe, that lived in Minnesota, from 1810 to 1863, also fought several wars against the invaders.

Initially, the government had Little Crow in high regard for his role in negotiations to transfer his tribe to a reservation near the Minnesota River. He accepted the *Sioux Crossing Treaty*, of 1851, persuading his tribe to follow him, because the promises of supplying goods to the natives, and guaranteeing some rights, seemed advantageous. However, little by little the federal government's commitments were no longer honored and in 1862 Little Crow complied with the Dakota War Council's decision by fighting against the white man. So he participated in the *Dakota War* that year, but decided to back down, before the end of the conflict, in December. On July 3, 1863, he was shot and killed by a settler.

Seattle. Chief Seattle, by whom one named after the capital of the State of Washington on the west coast, was of the Duwamish tribe, and although his nation is not as widely spoken as Sioux, Cherokee, and Apache, Seattle is recognized as a great leader and great warrior by the battles he fought along the Green River. Born in 1780 on the banks of the Black River, near the present-day city of Kent, he was baptized into the Catholic Church by the name of Noah. He died on June 7, 1866.

What gave prominence to Chief Seattle, among so many leaders who fought against the Euro-descendants in defense of lands inherited from the ancestors, was not a battle, or a campaign of war, but a speech, in March 1854, in which he called attention to the need to preserve the environment. In this speech, which he uttered while resting his hands on the shoulders of Governor Isaac Ingalls Stevens, he thanked the generosity of the Euro-descendants, but vehemently collected guarantees of access to land by the natives.

At the beginning of his speech he said: "The president in Washington sends word expressing the desire to buy our land. But how can anyone buy or sell heaven, earth? The idea is strange to us. If we do not have the property of air freshness and water flicker, how can anyone buy them? Every part of the earth is sacred to my people".

Sacagawea. But not just male leaders made the history of the Native Americans. A few years after the birth of Chief Seattle, now in 1788, the second most notable woman among the natives of the United States, Sacagawea, who was a guide and whose name is less famous only than that of Pocahontas, was born. It was of the Agaidika tribe, or "Salmon Eaters" tribe, of the Shoshone branch, and in 1800 she was kidnapped by men of the Hidatsa tribe, thus provoking a battle between the two nations. After several deaths of adults and children as a result of that fight, she was taken to what is now the city of Washburn, North Dakota.

There, still young, she married Toussaint Charbonneau, and was pregnant with her first child, in 1804, when her husband was approached by Lewis and Clark, who were trying to hire a guide for their historic expedition.

The *Lewis & Clark Expedition* hired Charbonneau, after dispensing several other suitors, because Sacagawea, the wife, spoke the Shoshone language, a skill necessary for the purposes of the endeavor.

The following year the expedition was begun, taking Sacagawea as a guide. Clark nicknamed her Janey. At a point, one of the boats turned, and Sacagawea used her ability to save various objects that were in it, including records of its own journey. Because of this, that watercourse was named a few months later as the Sacagawea River.

Not only because she was an interpreter, but also because she was a native and feminine figure, she is seen as the predominant factor for the expedition to have been well successful, without having been attacked or considered a threat by the tribes it encountered at way.

Revived today as a symbol in the struggle for women's rights, Sacagawea is honored with several statues in various locations throughout the United States.

Crazy Horse. However, the Lewis & Clark Expedition was not completely free of setbacks. At one point she was prevented from proceeding, blocked by a group of Lakota Sioux natives, who did not allow incursions into their lands, even for study purposes. One of the leaders of this blockade was the father of the future Chief Crazy Horse, Black Buffalo. This happened to be also the name of the woman of Crazy Horse, Black Buffalo Woman. Crazy Horse, who lived from 1840 to 1877, fought alongside Sitting Bull when he defeated General Custer. Younger, he took the place of supporting actor in the battle, reason why his name does not have so much projection as the name of that leader.

However, in June 1876, Crazy Horse was the one who initiated the *Sioux War*, attacking and defeating, with 1,500 men, the troops of General George Crook, who later had to fight under the orders of General Custer. And the greatest of the fights against Custer was rightly undertaken by Crazy Horse, on January 8, 1877, at the *Battle of Wolf Mountain*, Montana.

On May 5, with his men already weakened, he surrendered in Nebraska to the man he had previously defeated, General Crook. While a prisoner, he was killed by a guard on September 5 of that year for attempted escape, according to what has been officially registered.

The figure of Crazy Horse is carved on Thunderhead Mountain, South Dakota, in work of 1947, by the sculptor Korezak Ziolkowski. The place had been chosen by the warrior's son in 1940.

Manuelito. Chief Manuelito, who lived from 1818 to 1893, gained renown for his struggles against invaders of the territories of his people, the Navajo tribe, and also for a very sad fact in the life of those natives, which was the *Long Walk*.

Married to Narbonne's daughter, Manuelito became chief of the Navajos in 1855. His father-in-law had been killed by soldiers in 1849, and two years later the Army built Fort Defiance in the Navajo area, receiving great opposition from the natives. Even so, when he became the leader of the tribe, he made great effort to reach an agreement with the federal government, and in 1855 he signed the *Meriwether Treaty*, which guaranteed peace between the army and his tribe.

In 1860, however, Army soldiers stole many of the Navajo's horses. The fact put an end to the peace period, because the Navajos saw it like a deliberate breach of the agreement. The fights then resumed. Followed by Chief Barboncito, Manuelito led a thousand warriors to try to recover the horses at Fort Defiance, but he was unsuccessful.

There followed a phase of several years of battles, in which the natives were losing strength, before the massive investment of the Army against them. In 1963 Manuelito met with General James Carleton, commander of the Army in the region, carrying a peace proposal. Carleton, however, demanded that Manuelito and his warriors sign the surrender and accept the transfer of the tribe to a reservation far removed from their traditional dwelling. Manuelito refused to accept those conditions.

In January of 1864 Carleston made a sudden attack against the Navajo, destroying homes, cattle, plantations and everything that was found ahead. In August, assisted by Colonel Christopher "Kit" Carson, of indigenous origin, he imposed on Manuelito the transfer of his people to the reservation of Bosque Redondo, which happened through the Long Walk, of almost 500 kilometers, that lasted 18 days from Arizona to Fort Sumner in eastern New Mexico. More than 300 Navajos died of starvation and inanition during the journey, with many of them having died drowned while crossing the Rio Grande. About 8,000 Navajos were settled in the reservation.

In 1868, Manuelito and other Navajo chiefs signed with the government the *Treaty of Bosque Redondo*, granting them freedom and even the redemption of part of their old lands. Through peaceful means, including meetings with President Grant and President Hayes, Manuelito continued the struggle for the recovery of the Navajo lands, but without much success.

In 1893, he died of pneumonia, in the Navajo reservation that had been established in New Mexico.

Benito Juarez. First indigenous president in the Americas, Benito Pablo Juarez Garcia lived between 1806 and 1872. Born in San Pablo Guelatao, Oaxaca, Mexico, in the Zapotec tribe, he was orphaned at the age of three and was raised by an uncle. She worked on corn crops and shepherded sheep until the age of 12, year 1818, when, still illiterate, he moved to the city of Oaxaca in search of conditions to study. His sister worked there as a cook and got him a domestic job. Antonio Salanueva, a Franciscan friar, was enchanted with the intelligence and the will power of the boy Benito and directed him to a seminary. There he studied, but instead of graduating in Theology, he preferred the career of Law. In 1834 he began to advocate and in 1842 became a judge of law. He ruled the State of Oaxaca from 1847 to 1853, when he had to go into exile in Louisiana, USA, for his criticism of corruption in the federal government of Antonio Lopez de Santa Anna.

When Santa Anna resigned in 1855, he returned to Mexico and became a minister of justice. In 1857, in the country's first direct presidential election, he was elected vice president (Mexico had ingenuously copied the ephemeral system that elected the coup leader Louis Bonaparte in France nine years earlier, sealing for the Aztec's country its destiny for poverty). Moved away, as interim president, by the conservatives of Felix Maria Zuloaga, he later prepared his return from Veracruz, and in 1861 was elected President of the Republic.

Of progressive liberal profile, he marked the history of Mexico not only for leading the civil war that overthrew and executed the brief Emperor Maximilian I (1863-1867), of the real house of Austria Habsburgs, imposed to the country by Louis Bonaparte, then Emperor Napoleon III of France, but also for having promoted an agrarian reform that gave title of property to small farmers from north to south.

After the fall of Maximilian I, he was again elected to the presidency, and once again re-elected, having served for four terms as president, beyond the initial period as interim, until he died in 1872, of apoplexy.

Satanta. Chief Satanta, of the Kiowa tribe, was born in 1820, on the banks of the Arkansas River, and died in October 1878, in Huntsville, Texas. His name comes from the word Kiowa Set'tainte, which means White Bear. He gained notoriety as a great negotiator in the defense of his tribe and allied tribes, playing a prominent role in drafting important treaties, such as *Little Arkansas* and *Medicine Lodge*. He has since then become known as the "Speaker of the Plains".

When the government ordered his tribe to transfer to a reservation, he agreed, but the tribe did not move. Then General Custer arrested him and held him hostage, until the Kiowa marched into the reservation, according to the government's decision.

In 1871, near Fort Zarah in Kansas, a young Kiowa was killed by men of the Army Cavalry. The tribe wanted to avenge the boy's death, but Satanta judged that he had no strength to do so, and sought to avoid war. However, at the end of the day the cavalry attacked the Kiowa camp and Satanta gathered the warriors to confront the government forces.

That same year Satanta led train attacks in Texas. In one such attack, on May 18, seven of the men on the train were killed, while five escaped. General William Tecumseh Sherman and Colonel Ranald S. Mackenzie were behind those responsible, which led to the arrest of the Chiefs Sitting Bear (*Satank*), Big Tree (*Ado-ete*) and Satanta. Sherman demanded the civil court trial of those three Kiowa chiefs, a novelty in the case of Indian chiefs. When they were boarded on the train, Sitting Bear reacted and after some clashes with the guards died shot. Big Tree and Satanta suffered condemnation, and Satanta was sentenced to hang. But the same judge who convicted him asked the governor to commute the sentence, which became a prison.

In 1973 Satanta and Big Tree were released on parole. Shortly afterwards the tribe promoted an attack on buffalo merchants and authorities accused Satanta of being the artificer of the event, which would violate his provisional freedom. The Kiowas ensured that the chief did not participate, but did not convince the government, which decreed his arrest. In October 1874 he surrendered and was taken to the Huntsville State Prison. While working as a prisoner in the construction of railways, Satanta was affected by illness and little by little his interest in life was hanging. On October 11, 1878, he jumped from the window of the penitentiary hospital, which was installed on an upper floor, dying immediately.

Quanah Parker. Chief Quanah Parker, of the Quahadi ("antelope") branch of the Comanche tribe, lived between 1845 and 1911, in Oklahoma. He was the son of Chief Peta Nocona and Cynthia Ann Parker, an Anglo-American who was kidnapped from among the settlers as a child. As a young man, he fought several battles against Colonel Mackenzie's men, often for the defense of the area where his tribe hunted buffaloes. In 1867 Quanah participated in the negotiations of the *Medicine Lodge Treaty*, in Kansas, which provided for the transfer to reservations of tribes such as Kiowa, Cheyenne and the Comanches themselves, but he refused to sign the document. In 1871, as stated above, the Army arrested the Kiowa Chiefs Sitting Bear, Big Tree and Satanta, and at that time the federal government recognized Quanah as chief of all Comanches, although he was never appointed to the post within the tribe.

In 1873, called for a Dance of the Sun, a Kiowa rite, by the Comanche shaman Isa-tai, Quanah's group was convinced, during that ceremony, that the true enemies of the Comanches were the buffalo merchants, and those were who they had to attack. In one of the battles that followed, Quanah was shot in the shoulder without much gravity. He was rescued and healed, but the fact led the Army to plan a solution to the problem. Then it happened the *Red River War*. The following year, in September 1874, Colonel Mackenzie's men shot down 1,500 Comanche horses, seen as the reason for the tribe's power. With his weakened people, without food and under army pressure, in 1875 Quanah surrendered and accepted the transfer of the tribe to the reservation that the government had already assigned to it. In 1911 Quanah died at his home, Star House, in the town of Cache, Oklahoma, for cardiac arrest caused by rheumatism. He is considered the last chief of the Comanches, since after him the position of leader happened to be considered chairman, or president, no longer chief.

Running Rabbit. Chief Running Rabbit (*Aatsista Mahkan*, in his tribe language), who lived between 1833 and 1911, was the leader of the Blackfoot tribe of Canada and gained notoriety for his generosity, his kindness, and the protection he gave to his family.

In 1877 he signed the *Treaty Number 7*, which provided for the transfer to a reservation, but his tribe continued in the traditional area, hunting bison, until in 1881 these animals ceased to exist in the region. Then the tribe went to the planned reservation, near Calgary, Alberta.

By the example of Chief Running Rabbit we can see that the relationship between the natives of Canada and the representatives of the government, always linked to the British crown, was much more peaceful than the natives of the United States with the federal government, and also of the their settlers. Somehow, by circumstances still to be studied, the British were more successful in dealing with the natives of North America than the rulers of Mexico, the post-independence United States, and the Dutch pioneers of New York, centuries earlier. Thus, many native chiefs of the United States have distinguished themselves as great warriors and have their names studied today by schoolchildren, very differently than in Canada.

Wilma Mankiller. The Cherokee leader Chief Wilma Pearl Mankiller, of Oklahoma, who lived between 1945 and 2010, therefore, in recent times, in which the natives of the United States who maintains their traditions are all living in reservations, was the daughter of a Cherokee native and a Euro-descendant, and gained prominence not only for being the first woman to lead her tribe, always militating in favor of women's rights, but also for fighting for better living conditions of the natives, in the areas of education, health and management, rejecting the policy proposed by the government to base the development of reservations on the release of casinos within them. In her management she restored the Cherokee high school, Sequoyan High School, and improved the relationship between the tribe and the federal government. After finishing her term as chief, she became a guest teacher at Darmouth College, and was honored with the 1998 Medal of Freedom by President Clinton. Recalling this award, in a speech at the time of her death, President Obama said, "She was recognized for her vision and her commitment to a brighter future for all Americans".

Many other chiefs, other than those cited above, have made history in the United States over the decades and centuries past, though not as famously as a Sitting Bull, a Crazy Horse, or a Tecumseh. Among them we remember *Little Turtle* (1752-1812, from the Miami tribe, Indiana), *Pontiac* (1720-1769, from the Ottowa tribe, Illinois), *Captain Jack* (1837-1873, from the Modoc tribe, California), *Joseph* (1840-1904, from the Nez Perce tribe, Wallowa branch, Oregon) and *Mangas Coloradas* ("Red Sleeves", 1790-1863, Apache tribe, Chiricahua branch, New Mexico).

9.
Returning to the South people

Senator Darcy Ribeiro, almost certainly the most committed Brazilian intellectual among the graduates of the University of Sao Paulo, used to say that he was a descendant of Afonso Ribeiro, the Portuguese sailor who, according to Pero Vaz de Caminha's April 1500 Letter, Pedro Alvares Cabral left among the natives of Porto Seguro, for having during the trip until Brazil caused many disagreements among his companions. If the senator's statement is true, Afonso Ribeiro is the father of the first mameluke (son of white and indigenous) born in Brazilian lands. Officially, however, such primacy belongs to another Portuguese navigator, also wrecked in Bahia, years later, as we will see below.

At least 94% of Brazil's population is descended from indigenous people, according to research recently released. Darcy Ribeiro, if his surname is really an inheritance of that Afonso of Porto Seguro, differs from the other compatriots for having as his grandmother, one ignores how many generations ago, the wife of a pioneer settler, of the fleet that came to take possession of the land in the name of King Dom Manuel I, as well as the poet Paulo Bonfim, prince of the Brazilian poets in this beginning of the 21st century, differs from the rest of the inhabitants of the country, since he assures that, according to his genealogical research, he is descended from Pero Dias, son-in-law of Chief Tibiriça.

Following the poet, after going through the chronicle concerning the Indians of the three Americas from the years of the Discoveries to the 21st century, let us return once more in time to recall what happened in the South.

According to historical accounts, the novice Pero was involved with Terebeh, one of the chief's daughters. The two young ones were sneaking around, until her father surprised them in moment of hugs and kisses. From what he had learned from the Jesuits, a novice from the Society of Jesus could not marry, which would make that courtship unworthy. The novice, however, asserted that he was willing to abandon religious life to marry Terebeh, baptized as Maria da Graca (Mary of Graces). As the vow of chastity had already been made, the problem was brought to the charge of the clergy in Sao Paulo of Piratininga, who was Father Manoel da Nobrega. He sent a delegation to Rome explaining that if Pero Dias's vow of chastity was not annulled, in order for him to marry, Tibiriça would expel all the Portuguese from the Plateau of Piratininga, and probably also from the coast. The general of the Order, Ignatius of Loyola, left the dilemma with the following conclusion: It is better to lose a novice than to lose America. He granted permission for the wedding, and so Pero left the cassock. Suzana Dias, daughter of the couple, is the founder of the city of Santana de Parnaiba, near the city of Sao Paulo, and the main street of the village, in front of the Mother Church, is called Suzana Dias Street.

After the wars moved by Pikeroby, against Sao Vicente Village and against his two brothers Tibiriça and Caiuby in the two Jesuit nuclei of the area that would become the municipality of Sao Paulo, that is, Piratininga and Jurubatuba, on the banks of the Tamanduateih River and the Jurubatuba River, now the Pinheiros River, there came a long period of peace between natives of the Southern Region of Brazil and the settlers who were arriving from Portugal.

Rio. Why did the Portuguese avoid Guanabara Bay?

Meanwhile, the eastern region of Brazil, in its southern part, lived in relative abandonment by the colonizers, who feared conflicts with the brave cannibal warriors of the place, the Tupinambas of Guanabara, and this occurred even after the founding of the city of Sao Salvador of Bahia, in the All Saints Bay (*Bahia de Todos os Santos*), in 1549, by the first governor-general of Brazil, Tome de Souza.

The choice of the All Saints Bay to install the capital of the colony was not the work of unsuspecting planners, but happened as a result of a maritime accident. Towards the end of 1509, a French vessel headed for Sao Vicente was shipwrecked on that coast. The Tupinamba killed the survivors who arrived on the beach, who seemed to be invaders, but later found a Portuguese sailor, who was part of the group, stretched out among the stones, with a lamprey aspect, a word that in Tupi is "Caramuru". Soon they shouted that word, Caramuru, which happened to be the nickname of that navigator, a nobleman named Diogo Alvares Correia. Perhaps because it did not represent a threat, due to the situation in which he was found, he was well treated and happened to marry a native woman baptized as Catarina. She was Catarina Paraguaçu, and helped her husband to found the town that today is the municipality of Cachoeira, neighbor of Salvador. When Tome de Sousa was sent by the court, he came to Bahia, because it was a place pacified by Caramuru thirty years ago, and there was no risk of finding rebel leaders, as it was the case of Pikeroby in the Captaincy of Sao Vicente.

Statue of Catarina Paraguaçu in Salvador-Brazil

To the south of Salvador, Cachoeira and Santa Cruz Cabralia, the Portuguese had some contact with Cabo Frio, a region dominated by the Tupinamba, but they avoided Guanabara Bay, inhabited by a fearsome branch of this tribe, famous for the practice of anthropophagy.

It was in these conditions that in 1554, on a secret visit to Cabo Frio, where many French merchants were doing business, the French sailor Nicolas Durand de Villegagnon, 44, a noble diplomat graduated in Law from the University of Paris, studied with his compatriots the possibility of establishing a military base in Guanabara Bay. To have more assurance that his plan would succeed, he also made contacts with indigenous people there.

On his return to France he made a four-hour explanation to King Henry II, convincing him of the correctness of the attack. At the end of that year, the monarch ordered Minister Gaspard de Coligny, who was still a Catholic at the time, to prepare a secret expedition to Guanabara Bay, with Villegagnon as commander.

With difficulty finding volunteers for the trip, Villegagnon visited prisons and obtained the adhesion of many inmates, who would gain the freedom in exchange of the participation in the expedition. He knew that the Portuguese had the practice of sending the exiles here, but the idea of bringing in detainees to live with his sailors on the new continent would be costly to him. In August 1555 he left with two ships, packed with 600 passengers, and a barge of groceries. Among other important figures, an Indian of the Tabajara tribe, who would be his interpreter, came with him; the French wife of this native; a Scottish bodyguard; the navigator Andre Thevet, who had already visited the Bay of Guanabara twice; Bois-le-Comte, who was his nephew; Nicolas Barre, former pilot and rapporteur of the expedition; and two Benedictines, who would create the first Catholic school in the city to be founded.

On November 10, 1555, they founded in the area known today as Flamengo Beach the town of Henriville, named after the late Henry II of France, although only months later, in 1556, after the installation of potteries, is that the construction of masonry buildings began. The city that stood there would serve as the capital of "France Antarctique", the colony Villegagnon promised to found for the French crown.

Calvinists. Did Villegagnon receive the requested reinforcements from France in the expected measure?

On February 12, Andre Thevet, accompanied by the governor Villegagnon's nephew, Bois-le-Comte, returned to France for having fallen ill in the colony and needing treatment. Their departure also had the purpose of asking the crown to send more Frenchmen to secure colonization. Villegagnon asked for 4,000 soldiers, laborers and also a few hundred women, to marry the French unmarried men already in the area and those who would arrive.

Two days after the departure of Andre Thevet and Bois-le-Comte the first rebellion between the French of Guanabara occurred. Thirty men led by a individual who had been forced to marry an indigenous woman planned the murder of Villegagnon. A guard whom they promised reward to facilitate the action acted against the rebels and denounced the plan. With the attempt failed, the leader fled, but some were arrested, and two of them were hanged.

The second reckless initiative of the Villegagnon enterprise, after the regimentation of prisoners, was the expulsion of the tribe that traditionally occupied the Governador Island, then Paranapuan Island. These were the Temiminoh natives, a Tupi branch, who were forced to leave the place by the Tamoios (from "tamuya", which in Tupi means "the eldest", the first of the place, the Tamoios were not a tribe but a confederation of Tupinambas), allied to the French leader. Chief Maracaja-Guaçu and his Temiminoh followers went north, obtaining welcome in the Captaincy of Espirito Santo.

While knowing the affective relationships between the French and the Tupinamba women, Villegagnon demanded marriage. Some agreed to marry, but others chose to live in the woods with their mates. Other Frenchmen returned to France sheltered in merchant ships.

At that time, Gaspard de Coligny was converted to Protestantism. Knowing the difficulties of securing substantial numbers of settlers in France Antarctique, he asked Calvin in Geneva to send a contingent of Protestants to Guanabara. Calvin obtained the consent of two pastors, who agreed to come with a certain number of faithful. Funded by Coligny and Villegagnon, the expedition departed from France on November 19, 1956, with a total of 300 people on three ships commanded by Bois-le-Comte. They arrived in Guanabara on February 26.

At the end of March Villegagnon wrote to Calvin, his old high school classmate, thanking him for his commitment and telling of his difficulties.

In a short time the pastors disagreed with the governor and at the beginning of 1558 they returned to France, taking many faithful with them. Of the Calvinists who remained, some rebelled and three of them were executed by the government of France Antarctique. Villegagnon had to return to France to explain his action in 1559, leaving Bois-le-Comte as interim governor.

Reintegration. What was the role of Estacio de Sa in the expulsion of the French?

France Antarctique was short-lived, not exceeding a dozen years, by its own geographical conformation. The Portuguese who had the possession of Brazil by the Treaty of Tordesillas, used to travel from Cabo Frio to Sao Vicente passing through the Guanabara Bay and simply left the Indians of that area in their customary life, without seeing much need to drop anchor there and risk their lives against the anthropophagous, since there was so much land to colonize in all the Brazilian coast. The arrival of Villegagnon was thus seen as an untimely invasion, and the expulsion of the French from that bay was a matter of organization and time.

The second governor-general of Brazil, Dom Duarte da Costa, died in 1558, having been replaced by the gentleman Mem de Sa, who was half-brother of the poet Sa de Miranda.

Villegagnon's departure for France in 1559 showed Mem de Sa two signs of opportunity. First, there was weakening of the French settlement. Second, that the leader's departure could have left the settlers of Guanabara with an open flank. Thus, relying on information from a French deserter, Jean de Coynta, he organized the first attack on France Antarctique in 1560.

The calculations were correct. The governor-general took the city, by means of the destruction of Fort Coligny, that Villegagnon had built, with French and indigenous labor, on the Island of Villegagnon, then Island of Serigipe. The defeated French, however, were not completely destructed, for they were welcomed by their allied Tamoios, with whom they remained hidden, as well as a number of settlers who moved to Cabo Frio to pretend to be merchants.

The years that followed were difficult for the Portuguese, who had to face hostilities of the Tamoios to the south and to the north of Guanabara Bay. In missionary work, Jose de Anchieta was arrested in the village of Iperoig, where today is the city of Ubatuba. For five months he was hostage to the warriors of the tribe, led by Chief Caoquira ("Bud of Leaf").

Manuel da Nobrega and Jose de Anchieta managed to negotiate a treaty with the Tamoios in 1563 so that they would not attack the Portuguese who operated south of Ubatuba and the Plateau of Piratininga. This was called *Peace of Iperoig*, the first peace treaty of the Americas, which guaranteed the continuity of catechesis and education in the Jesuit colleges of Sao Paulo and the region of Santos.

Born in 1500, Mem de Sa saw that he needed young blood to face the rest of the French and Tamoio resistance. He asked that his nephew, Estacio de Sa, was sent from Portugal, and this one, coming to Salvador in 1563, arrived in Guanabara Bay in March 1565 and created the city of Sao Sebastiao do Rio de Janeiro, between the Cara de Cao Hill and the Sugarloaf Mountain, to function as the basis of his military operations.

After several battles, with the help of the governor of the Captaincy of Sao Vicente and the indigenous Temiminohs, now headed by Chief Arariboia, son of Maracaja-Guaçu, Estacio de Sa secured the definitive possession of the area in 1567, although he was wounded in battle, struck by a poisoned arrow, and died a month later, on February 20 of that year, at the age of 47. As a prize for support in the struggle, Arariboia gained possession of a vast sesmaria, east of Rio, where he founded the city of Niteroi.

Pacification. Why did the Corurupe River Massacre occur?

Mem de Sa still had to face during his administration, which followed until 1572, year of his death, some wars against indigenous tribes, like the battle against the Tupiniquins of Ilheus, in 1559, and the attack given by the aimores to Caravelas and Porto Seguro, and also to Ilheus, in 1564. The aimores still returned to face the settlers even in the beginning of the Spanish dominion, as it was the attack of

1597 to Porto Seguro, but the clashes with the natives in that period were punctual and rare.

This conflict of 1559 was the most striking case among the attacks of Indians against settlers in the region that is now the State of Bahia. The episode was known as the *Battle of the Swimmers*, and, on the side of the anti-Portuguese, also like Massacre of the Corurupe River, for the event to have happened in the mouth of this river and by the great number of casualties imposed to the natives by the colonizers. It was a farm owned by Mem de Ss himself. It happened in it the murder of one of the natives and the measures that these natives claimed were not taken for the investigation of the case. They then decided to promote a mutiny. When the men of the governor-general arrived, the natives entered the sea, swimming. The soldiers also swam, and, in greater numbers, they killed large quantity of natives. The rest surrendered.

Somehow, the Spanish crown had with the natives of Brazil, from 1580, a more pleasant relationship than that established here by the Portuguese.

This phase of tranquility that came was broken when, in the following century, the Bandeirantes were divided between those who sought ores in the backlands and those who went hunting for Indians to be sold as slaves. On the south side, the wars were then restarted, as we have already seen above, when these adventurers decided to imprison acculturated Guarani residents in the Reductions of what is now the State of Rio Grande do Sul, with the Battle of M'Borore in 1641, and in other part, the Northeast, with the natives helping the Portuguese to expel invaders.

Dutch. What action has taken the Pernambuco mill owners to revolt against the Dutch Domain?

A few years before establishing the colony of New Holland, now New York, in North America, the Dutch took advantage of the apparent abandonment of the Spanish crown over the area of Brazil and promoted some invasions. They formed a colony in Pernambuco in 1630, after having tried to take Bahia in an unsuccessful enterprise, in 1624.

This invasion in Salvador, Bahia, lasted from May 1624 to May

1625. Governor-General Diogo de Mendonca Furtado resisted within the palace, but was captured and sent to Holland. The governor of Pernambuco, Matias de Albuquerque, was then appointed by Spain as governor-general of Brazil, and began to administer the colony from the then Pernambuco capital, which was the city of Olinda. Albuquerque sent soldiers to try to regain Bahia, but it was only when Madrid sent an armada of 52 ships and 12,000 men, on the so-called *Vassal Journey*, that the Dutch were finally defeated and expelled.

Years later, a successful sack of the annual silver shipment of the colonies to Spain, on the so-called *Beach Fleet*, in the Caribbean Sea, by Admiral Piet Hein, strengthened the Dutch and provided funds for the organization of a new attempt, occurred with the invasion of Olinda in 1630.

From the base of Pernambuco, Dutch power extended with the capture of Rio Grande do Norte and Paraiba in 1634, Ceara in 1637, and the capital of Maranhao, Sao Luiz, in 1641.

In 1637, the entourage of Count John Maurice of Nassau-Siegen, future Prince Maurice of Nassau, arrived in Pernambuco to direct the already vast Dutch Brazil, establishing the capital of his colony in the city of Recife. He was a man of open and modernizing vision, and there he established a botanical garden, a zoological garden, a thriving sugar industry, the culture of religious freedom, and the practice of incentive to arts, including Architecture. Under the rule of Nassau the first synagogue of the Americas was founded in Recife. Nassau also intensified the arrival of black slaves, to work in sugarcane plantations and mills. In Europe he lived surrounded by scientists and artists, some of whom he brought to Recife, such as the painters Frans Post and Albert Eckhout. The scientist Rene Descartes was part of his army in the Netherlands, but he suffered of asthma and did not come to Brazil.

Newly emancipated from Spain, since 1581, having developed in Protestantism, unlike the Iberian Union, the Netherlands sought to incorporate part of the territories that its former colonizer gained from the union with Portugal in 1580, and which kept under a certain vacuum of power. The Spanish government only came to recognize

Dutch independence in 1648, with the *Munster Peace Agreement*, and until that year it prohibited, as retaliation, that the Spaniards did trade in the Dutch ports, which made it difficult, for example, to acquire sugar.

Bahia, first coveted point, proved faithful to the Iberian power and it was not there that the Netherlands managed to set up their base. Navigating further north, they found it relatively easy to conquer almost the entire territory that would become the Northeast region of Brazil. The Dutch, as good merchants they are, were able to gain the support of the natives, bringing from Europe the industrialized products they valued, such as scissors, knives, pistols, mirrors and spoons, and took in exchange cotton, fish, wood and minerals, among others goods.

After the dismemberment of the Portuguese and Spanish crowns, in 1640, the colonial leaders of Brazil began to articulate the struggle for the expulsion of the Dutch. The city of Sao Luiz was rescued in 1644, but the other provinces that they formed only managed to be definitively free of the Dutch power ten years later, in 1654.

There were many battles, which united Portuguese, indigenous people and black, against the Dutch settlers.

At first, Matias de Albuquerque settled in Arraial do Bom Jesus, near Recife, to organize the resistance. But the mill owners, who moved the captaincy economy, gradually joined the Dutch administration, seeing advantages in the new style of power. The spokesman of these businessmen in front of the Dutch government was Domingos Fernandes Calabar, who happened to act like enemy of the deposed governor.

In 1635, the Arraial do Bom Jesus was conquered by the Dutch, which led Matias de Albuquerque to move away and set up his new base of operations on the banks of the Sao Francisco River.

In 1641 the governments of Portugal and Holland signed the *Luso-Dutch Treaty*, which provided for a truce for ten years. As a result, in 1643 the Dutch crown requested the presence of Nassau in Europe, promising him important new duties.

The new administration of the Dutch domain in Recife began to collect back taxes from the mill owners, which resulted in the so-called *Pernambucan Insurrection*, in 1645, and led some to seek composition with those who fought for the return of Portuguese rule. Two of these businessmen, Andre Vidal de Negreiros and Joao Fernandes Vieira, joined the rebel leader Henrique Dias, the son of former slaves, and the indigenous leader Antonio Filipe Camarao, the Potiguaçu, doing to recrudesce the struggle for the expulsion of the Dutch, campaign that became known as the *War of Divine Light*.

The bloodiest episodes of this struggle were the first and second *Battles of Guararapes*, in April 1648 and February 1649. The Brazilian Army considers these two battles as the basis of its formation.

However, it was only five years later, on January 26, 1654, that the invaders were definitively defeated, with the signature of the document known as *Capitulation of Campo do Taborda*, in which the Supreme Council of Recife officially handed over to General Francisco Barreto de Menezes, named governor of the Captaincy of Pernambuco, the possession of Recife, then called Mauritius City, and other occupied colonies, such as the Fernando de Noronha Archipelago, Itamaraca Island, Rio Grande do Norte, Ceara and Paraiba.

Figures. What was the most remarkable indigenous war in the South American East?

As we have done above, while recording the profile of several native chiefs of North America, we now proceed to create a modest gallery of noteworthy people from South America, among natives and children of natives. We will not deal only with the war chiefs, for in the eastern south, except for the attacks of Pikeroby, the Guarani War, the battles against the French in Guanabara, some attacks in Bahia against Mem de Sa and his successor, and the wars against the Dutch, most of the great Indian characters gained prominence by other deeds and other circumstances. In the Pacific, the confrontation was very bloody between natives and Spaniards, and we will deal with this soon, while we are talking about some famous names.

Catarina Paraguaçu. Born probably in 1495, she was the daughter of Chief Taparica, of the Tupinambas of Bahia, and before the arrival of the Portuguese in the Reconcavo, according to Fray Jose de Santa Rita Durao, in his epic poem "Caramuru", of 1781, she was called Guaibimpara ("Owner of the Sea"). However, even though she is the daughter of the chief, the name may have been created in the poem by the influence of romanticism, since it does not fit with the view of property of the natives. At the decision of his father, she married Diogo Alvares Correia, Caramuru - the Portuguese nobleman who was saved from shipwreck in the domain of the tribe in 1509 -, and was baptized in 1528, in France, under the name Catarina of Brazil. The name Paraguaçu ("Big Sea") may have been incorporated into it as a surname in allusion to the Paraguaçu River, the largest river that flows into the All Saints Bay, but may also have been her childhood name. She and Caramuru formed, officially, the first Christian family in Brazil, and Americas, and she is considered as the symbolic mother of the Brazilian motherland. He died on January 26, 1583.

Atahualpa. The last Inca emperor, Atahualpa ("Bird of Fortune", in Quechua) lived between 1500 and 1533. His father, Emperor Hayna Capac, died in 1527, of smallpox, after contact with Spaniards. Without having left an indicated successor, the two sons with more recognized leadership, Huascar and Atahualpa, divided the kingdom, with the first being crowned Inca emperor in Cusco and the second organizing the Inca army of the north, based in Quito. Huascar, also named Tupac Cusi Huallpar, born in 1491, was governor of Cusco, while Atahualpa was governor of Quito, both previously named by his own father. With the dispute for the central throne, it broke out the Inca Civil War, which finished in 1532, with victory of Atahualpa.

When he traveled with his men from Cajamarca to Cusco, to be crowned emperor of the whole Inca Empire, Atahualpa was surprised by a Spanish expedition, which was under the orders of Francisco Pizarro. Captured by Pizarro, Atahualpa offered him a large prize to be released, which was accepted.

Atahualpa, however, did not gain freedom, for the Spaniards feared being attacked by the Incas. They accused the new monarch of treason against the Spanish crown and for having murdered Huascar, of whom he was a half-brother. He was submitted to a court of justice and sentenced to death, executed by strangulation, on July 26, 1533.

Pizarro named as successor of Atahualpa another Indian, Tupac Hualpa, but this one was assassinated next. That same year 1533 Pizarro gave inauguration to Manco Inca Yupanqui, another son of Hayna Capac, but this rebelled against the Spaniards in 1536 and, defeated, was plunged in the forest, being replaced in the throne by another brother, Paullu Inca, who collaborated with the Spaniards until his death in 1549. Meanwhile, Manco Inca Yupanqui created a dynasty in Vilcabamba, having been succeeded by his sons Sayn Tupac Inca, Titu Cusi Yupanqui and Tupac Amaru I, who was on the throne when the Spaniards took over the territory, in 1572. In any case, Atahualpa is considered as the last Inca emperor.

Inca Emperor Huascar

Ines (Agnes) Huaylas Yupanqui. Sister of Atahualpa, the Inca princess Ines Huaylas Yupanqui, whose original name was Quispe Sisa, lived between 1518 and 1559.

As part of Atahualpa's baffled rescue prize, she was taken to Cajamarca at the age of 18, and the emperor, while a prisoner of Pizarro, offered her to him to marry her. "Take the daughter of my father, my sister, whom I greatly care for", he would have told the old Spanish conquistador.

Pizarro took her as his wife, always presenting her so, and with her he had his daughter Francisca Pizarro Yupanqui, in 1534, and his son Gonzalo, in 1535. In 1536, when Manco Inca Yupanqui's rebellion in Cusco occurred, Ines was accused of passing information and of trying to flee, carrying chests of gold and silver. Pizarro then separated from her and then married Angelina Yupanqui, also Atahualpa's sister and daughter of Huayna Capac, having with her his son Francisco Pizarro Yupanqui.

Tibiriça. Chief Tibiriça ("Vigilant of the Mountain"), of the Tupiniquim tribe of the Plateau of Piratininga, Guaianas branch, was born around 1470 and died in 1562. He was married to Potyra. On the coast, his brother Pikeroby rescued the Portuguese navigator Joao Ramalho, who became his son-in-law, marrying Mbicy, later named Isabel, but called of Bartira by the Portuguese. Another daughter, Terebeh, married Pero Dias, and the third, Beatriz, married another Portuguese, Lopo Dias. Besides the three daughters, Tibiriça also had five sons: Italo, Ara, Toruih, Arata and Pirija.

Already set with the world of Europeans, through Joao Ramalho, he received in Piratininga, village of Napuambuçu, now central region of the city of Sao Paulo, the Jesuits who came up from the coast to found a school of first letters and catechesis.

After being educated by Leonardo Nunes and Jose de Anchieta, the chief was baptized with the name of Martim Afonso Tibiriça, in honor of the donee of the captaincy. Many important Brazilians in history were or are his descendants, as it is the case of Queen Silvia of Sweden.

For his support to the Jesuits and the Portuguese immigrants, he had to face warlike attacks by his brother Pikeroby and also the son of this, Jaguaranho, or Jaguanharoh.

He died on the Christmas day of 1562, afflicted by a plague that devastated the village, as narrated by Jose de Anchieta.

Arariboia. It is known that Chief Arariboia ("Ferocious Snake"), from the Temiminoh tribe, branch Tupinamba of the Governador Island, then Paranapuan, died in 1589, but does one not have an estimate of the date of his birth. He was also given the name of Martim Afonso when he was baptized in 1568, after having secured the previous year, with his bravery, the victory of Estacio de Sa on the French troops that occupied the Guanabara Bay.

In the bloodiest confrontation, which was the *Battle of Uruçumirim*, on the Hill of Gloria, the participation of Arariboia was decisive. Climbing up the rocks, he entered alone into the camp where the Frenchmen and Tamoios were. With a torch he carried, he blew up the powder warehouse, leaving his enemies with little ammunition and disoriented. It was in this battle that Estacio de Sa suffered the arrow that wounded him in the face and took him to the death weeks later, but the defeat of the French began to be drawn that day.

As a reward for his support, the Portuguese government presented him with the lands where the neighborhood of Sao Cristovao is today. The government also granted him the title of knight of the Order of Christ and gave him a set of garments that had belonged to King Dom Sebastiao. In 1573 he received the sesmaria of Sao Lourenco, where he founded the city of Niteroi, a name that in Tupi means "true cold river" (y = river, etei = true, roi = cold). In 1575, when the new governor-general of the southern section of the State of Brazil was inaugurated (Brazil would later be divided into State of Brazil and State of Maranhao), Antonio Salema, Arariboia crossed his legs while sitting, and this was seen by the chief of government as a sign of disrespect, without taking into account cultural differences. Since then he has lost credibility with the Portuguese, keeping away from government business until he died drowned in 1589.

Isabel de Jaguaripe. Died in 1585, there is neither the year of birth nor the Tupi name of the indigenous Isabel, who worked as a slave in the Bahia Reconcavo. Just as black slaves escaping into the woods formed the *quilombos*, the Indians created nuclei called *sanctities*, to shelter natives fleeing slavery and also from Jesuit missions that they did not adapt. A native named Antonio was one of those, who one day fled the mission of the Island of Tinhareh and founded on the continent the Jaguaripe Sanctity.

Fernao Cabral de Taide, an ill-intentioned master of sugar mill, managed to lure the community of Antonio to his lands, while promising that the natives would be free and protected. Isabel was one of the natives of the Jaguaripe Sanctity, who had taken refuge there after fleeing slavery.

One day she was accused of reporting extramarital affairs of Taide to his wife, Margarida da Costa. Taide then ordered the clerk, Domingos Camacho, to burn her alive at a bonfire. The overseer followed the order, aided by a Guinean slave.

Before the repercussion of the case, in the same year of 1585 the governor of Bahia, Tales Barreto, determined the dismantling of that sanctity. In 1591, during the visit of the Holy Office to Bahia, the episode was brought to the attention of the inquisitor, Heitor Furtado de Mendonca. As an aggravating circumstance, Paula Almeida also denounced Taide for sexually molesting her sister, who was twice a midwife to that master of sugar mill. Condemned by the Tribunal of the Holy Office, and given to the secular arm, according to the praxis of the time, Taide was taken to the bonfire, suffering the same type of death that had applied to Isabel six years before.

Cunhambebe. Born in an unknown year, Cunhambebe ("Chest of a Flat Woman", according to Professor Eduardo Navarro) died in 1555 after contracting a contagious disease, probably smallpox. He was the Tupinamba chief whom the German explorer Hans Staden says he has known in the region of Trindade, south of Parati. Also known by Andre Thevet, he allied himself with the French when Villegagnon arrived in Guanabara Bay in 1555. He began the formation of the Tamoios Confederation, which united about 70,000 Indians in coastal villages, or near the coast, in area that went from Cabo Frio, State of Rio de Janeiro, to Bertioga, State of Sao Paulo. A very feared warrior, one has spread his fame of having devoured at least 60 Portuguese in anthropophagy rituals, which, according to Darcy Ribeiro, by the belief of the Brazilian cannibals, had the function of transferring to the body of the diner the strength of the downed warrior. All the Tupinambas were allied to Cunhambebe in that great confederation. Capistrano de Abreu assures that there was a second Cunhambebe, son of the first, and that it was this son who negotiated with Jose de Anchieta in Ubatuba the Peace Treaty of Iperoig.

Aimberei. Died at the Battle of Uruçumirim, on January 20, 1567, Chief Aimberei ("Inflexible") forged his warrior phlegm when he was arrested, along with his father, Chief Cairuçu ("Wooden Honey"), of the Tupinamba of that region, which today is Flamengo Beach, and were brought to Sao Paulo of Piratininga by the men of the founder of Santos, Bras Cubas, to work as slaves on that owner's farms. Cairuçu fell ill and died in a short time, and the young Aimberei took advantage of the movement around the funeral of his father to escape. On this return trip he passed through the villages along the path, from Ubatuba. He visited several tribes along the coast, heading towards the Guanabara Bay. His objective was to create a confederation with these Tupinambas branches, which was realized in 1554 and happened to be known as the Tamoios Confederation, having as first leader Chief Cunhambebe, of Angra dos Reis. The animosity of Cairuçu, Cunhambebe and Aimberei in relation to the Portuguese developed in the resistance to the invaders of the colonists of the Captaincy of Sao Vicente, who hunted Tupinambas of those villages to enslave in the sugar cane farms.

With the death of Cunhambebe in 1555, immediately Aimberei was chosen chief of the Confederation.

It was Aimberei who persuaded Jaguanharoh to fight against the Portuguese and to try to convince his uncle Tibiriça to embrace the same cause, which resulted in the death of this son of Pikeroby at the hands of the chief of Piratininga when attacking the place in 1562. And it was also Aimberei who offered to take from Ubatuba to Sao Vicente a letter from Father Manuel da Nobrega to the governor of the captaincy, with guidelines for the armistice. He was accompanied by the Genoese Jose Adorno. Chief Caoquira had summoned to Ubatuba the main leaders of the Tamoios Confederation, including his brother Pindobuçu ("Big Palm") and Aimberei, for the conference with the Jesuits. As Aimberei and Adorno were slow to return, Manuel da Nobrega decided to go to Sao Vicente, leaving Anchieta in Ubatuba as a hostage. After months, Cunhambebe, the son, who was also there, decided to go with Anchieta to Sao Vicente. The talks with the governor happened to fruition, and many natives were released, including Igaraçu ("Big Canoe"), the fiancée of Aimberei.

Aimberei was maintained like chief of the Tamoios Confederation until being defeated and died in 1567, in the war of expulsion of the French of the Guanabara Bay.

Inacio Abiaru. Chief of one of the Guarani tribes settled in the Jesuit Missions of Rio Grande do Sul, Inacio Abiaru ("Black Thrush Bird") was designated by the leaders of his people as captain general of War and Major Justice, to confront the Bandeirantes that went to the region to imprison Indians to sell as slaves. At the Battle of M'Borore, in 1641, leading 4,000 Guaranis, and using cannons made of wooden trunks, plus a reduced number of rifles, he defeated the men of Jeronimo Pedroso de Barros, who had thousands of descendants of Portuguese and also Tupi of the Plateau of Piratininga.

In the year 1642 Abiaru stormed the fortresses of Apiterebi and Tobarati, where he freed more than a thousand Guarani who were captive.

There is no record of the years of birth and death of this victorious Guarani chief.

Potiguaçu. Leader Poty, or Potiguaçu ("Great Shrimp"), was from the Potiguara tribe of Rio Grande do Norte, and was born in the area of the current city of Ceara Mirim, in the outskirts of Natal, around 1590, and died in Recife on August 24, 1648. Baptized in 1614, in Extremoz, State of Rio Grande do Norte, he received the Christian name of Antonio, but also added the name Filipe, as a tribute to King Philip II, written currently as "Felipe" by Spaniards, but at the time as "Filipe", now officially treated as *Antonio Filipe Camarao* (Camarao is Shrimp in Portuguese).

He received careful instruction from the Jesuits and was respected as a good cultivator of the Portuguese language, both speaking and writing, and also mastering the basic Latin.

Soon after the arrival of the Dutch to Pernambuco, he integrated the army of the deposed governor, Matias de Albuquerque. He was the main and most valiant of the indigenous leaders to assist the Portuguese in the battles for the expulsion of the Dutch invader, sometimes accompanied by his wife, an exalted knight, with command of the spear and bow.

He excelled in the battles of *Mata Redonda*, *Porto Calvo* and *Sao Lourenco*. He then had a decisive role in the first Battle of Guararapes, in 1648, which earned him the honor of being treated as a "Dom", as a knight in the Order of Christ, the "nobleman with a coat of arms" and the title of "Chief captain of all the Indians of Brazil". However, he did not have time to enjoy these honors, for he died a month later as a result of injuries sustained in battle. His nephew, Diogo Pinheiro Camarao, succeeded him in the leadership of the indigenous soldiers.

Clara Camarao. Indigenous woman of the Tabajara tribe, who, for some scholars, was Potiguara, like Potiguaçu, or Antonio Filipe Camarao, Clara Camarao received Jesuit instruction with Potiguaçu as his colleague. While receiving the baptism together with him, they decided to get married that same day. Called Clara, she adopted the surname attributed to her husband. Born around 1595, she survived her husband's death in 1648, but there is no news of her trajectory after the pacification of the Captaincy of Pernambuco, once what is known of her came from the records left by him. Historians from Rio Grande do Norte and Pernambuco have investigated large numbers of documents, trying to find more data about her, for now without success. They hope that the translation of Dutch texts of the time will bring some light on this figure.

In the fight against the Dutch, women were forbidden to accompany the warrior husbands in some major battles, which led Clara to set up an exclusively female squad, which later became known as "Heroines of Tejecupapo".

It is said that on one occasion a detachment of Dutch people from Olinda was going to a well-known indigenous village, which was to be looted. The men of the tribe mounted a roadblock, but they were killed. When the Dutch reached the village, they were intercepted by the women, led by Clara. None of them continued alive.

Cangapol. Chief Cangapol, who lived between 1670 and 1757, nicknamed "Nicolas el Bravo", was leader of the northern Tehuelche tribe, who lived in the province of Buenos Aires, south of the Salado River. He gained renown for his great bravery and his cruelty, as well as his stature, which exceeded two meters, an unusual thing among the South American natives.

At the time of the Guarani War, Cangapol acted further south, promoting attacks on the Spaniards. Among his accomplishments it is the episode in which he led the largest assault war ("malon") to the city of Buenos Aires in the eighteenth century, when he sought to avenge the death of Chief Tolmichilla, his cousin, murdered in 1737 by a Spaniard. For the attack he added to the Tehuelches several other tribes, among them the Huiliches and the Pehuenches.

He was a friend of several Jesuits, but he disagreed with the policy of the Society of Jesus to join the natives in Reductions. He had initially supported the formation of the Mission of Our Lady of Pilar de Puelches, near Mar del Plata, by the Jesuits Thomas Falkner and Jose Cardiel. His tribe made commerce with residents of the Reduction, exchanging for brandy and tobacco its products of extractivism, hunting and fishing. He preferred to keep his people in the nomadic style of life, and over time he resented losing leadership among smaller caciques, welcomed by the Jesuits. In 1750 he decided to attack and abolish that settlement.

The language of his tribe, Aonikenk, is now almost extinct, spoken by only a few people, with the intense miscegenation of the Tehuelches with the Mapuches, of dominant culture in the region, being one of the reasons. The Tehuelche word itself, which gives name to the tribe, is of Mapuche origin, and means "brave people", because the Tehuelche tribe, also called "Patagonia", has the original name of "Aoniken".

The chief's name seems to be a composition of a Tupi-Guarani word (Canga, meaning "head", or "bone within the body") with an Aonikenk word (Pol, meaning "black"), since this language contains the letter "L", which does not exist in Tupi-Guarani.

In 1753 Cangapol became an ally of the Spaniards in the struggle against the Mapuches and other tribes that fought attacks trying to take control of the territory of the Pampas. There are no reports of the circumstances of his death, in 1757. His son Nicholas succeeded him as chief of the Tehuelches.

From this stage, mid-eighteenth century, South America, very unlike Yankee America, was relatively calm in its interaction with Euro-descendants, blacks and Indians. The reason for this peace lies almost entirely in the intense miscegenation of Spaniards and Portuguese with the Indians found here, so that almost everywhere along the Atlantic coast, from Sao Luiz do Maranhao, Brazil, to Rio

Gallegos, Argentina, there is a profusion of indigenous descendants, mixed with Europeans and blacks, but natives without miscegenation are found only far from the coast. Among the few exceptions it is the north coast of the State of Sao Paulo, which, before the Rio-Santos Highway, built in the 1970s, maintained many communities of isolated natives called Caiçaras (Caiçara = "wood palisade"), remnants of the Tupinamba of the Tamoios Confederation.

Today, even among them, there are few who did not mix, but they still exist. In the city of Sao Paulo, to the south, there are two Guarani villages, from the Mbya branch, formed by natives who came from the coast at the beginning of the twentieth century, climbing the mountain range from Itanhaem to selling handicrafts in the state capital. Many of them, at the time of their return, stopped to rest before the descent of the mountain range, where now is the district of Marsilac, Parelheiros region. The owner of these lands, a Japanese man who had no descendants, ceded the area to the Guarani, so they could stay there longer. Today they form the *Tekoa* ("village") Tenonde Poran ("beautiful future") and the Tekoa Krukutu (Koru = "gravel", Kutu = "to drill"). In these communities there are people mixed with non-native people, but most of them are indigenous people, unmixed. Also in the Jaragua Peak, still within the municipality of Sao Paulo, other Guarani have joined and formed, more recently, the Tekoa Pyau. Other indigenous groups, protected by Funai (National Indian Foundation), exist in the city of Sao Paulo, but are immigrants from places where there are no more original natives, but "caboclos", mixed descendants, who speak nothing of the language of their native ancestors. It is the situation of almost all the tribes of the vast Brazilian coast.

Candido Rondon. Seven years before the death of Benito Juarez, Mexico, the mestizo Candido Mariano da Silva Rondon, better known as Marshal Rondon, was born in Mimoso, municipality of Santo Antonio de Leverger, State of Mato Grosso, on May 5, 1865. He died in Rio de Janeiro on January 19, 1958. His father was a Portuguese descendant and his mother was an Indian, a descendant of the Bororo and Terena tribes.

His parents died early and he was raised by an uncle. When he was sixteen, he also lost his uncle, and moved to Rio de Janeiro. Already with high school completed, he taught for two years in elementary school, then entering the military career. He was a member of the 3rd Cavalry Regiment and graduated as a second lieutenant at the officers' school in 1888. At the War College he graduated in Mathematics, Physics and Natural Sciences.

Working as a military engineer, he participated in the construction of the highway connecting the city of Rio de Janeiro to Cuiaba, Mato Grosso. From 1890 to 1895 he led the implantation of telegraph lines from the then capital of the late Republic, Rio de Janeiro, to his state, Mato Grosso. At the beginning of the twentieth century, after pacificating the natives of the Bororo tribe, he had the help of these to continue the installation of the telegraph lines, managing to extend them to Bolivia and Peru.

Always bearing the motto "Die if you must, but never kill", he continued his work of pacifying native tribes. When commissioned to take the telegraph from Mato Grosso to the Amazon, he discovered the Juruena River, a tributary of the Tapajos, and in that region made contact with the Nambiquara tribe, who until that time had killed every white man who had tried to approach.

In May 1909 he led an expedition to explore the Madeira River. When they reached the Ji-Parana River, they were already without food, and then they were determined to live on what they got from the forest, hunting, fishing, and extractivism. They reached the Madeira River on December 25 of the same year. On the way he discovered another important watercourse, which he called the River of Doubt, and which today is the Roosevelt River. Returning to Rio de Janeiro, he was greeted as a hero, because the Army already gave him as dead. At that time he founded the SPI, Service of Protection to the Indians, today Funai, National Foundation of the Indian.

Accompanied by Theodore Roosevelt, former president of the United States, Rondon began the Rondon-Roosevelt Scientific Expedition in 1914, to explore the course of the River of Doubt. It was a difficult job, with many cases of illness and setbacks on the way. After this adventure is that the river received the name it has today.

While having participated in 1889 in the movement that led to the Proclamation of the Republic, in 1924 he led the attack against the rebellion of the State of Sao Paulo, guaranteeing with his troops the maintenance of federal power. Before the uncertainties of the Revolution of 1930, that year he left the presidency of the SPI, but returned to the post in 1939. In the late 1950s, he supported and advised the Villas-Boas brothers in the creation of the Xingu National Park, the first indigenous park of Brazil, installed in 1961. At that time he already had the rank of marshal, obtained in 1955, the highest of the Brazilian Army at the time.

The meridian of 52° west of Greenwich is named after Rondon Meridian, in honor of his work in communications. She is the second person in the world to receive this honor. In addition he has the title of "Father of Brazilian Telecommunications" and has his name inscribed in letters of gold in the Book of the Geographical Society of New York.

Raoni Metuktire. Born in 1930 in Mato Grosso, Chief Raoni ("Great Warrior" in Tupi, "Sex of Jaguar" in Kayapo), from the Metuktire branch of the Kayapo tribe, gained a reputation for his fight, including many international trips, in favor of the preservation of the Amazon Forest. His first contact with the Euro-descendants was in 1954 and his knowledge of the Portuguese language came from his friendship with the wilderness expert ("sertanista") Orlando, the oldest of the three Villas-Boas brothers. At the time of the contact he was already wearing his botoque, the wooden disc embedded in the lower lip, according to the tradition of his people.

In 1964 he received in his village the visit of King Leopold III of Belgium, in an expedition made to know Indian reservations of Mato Grosso. It began the international projection of the name of that chief.

In 1978, Jean-Pierre Dutilleux released the documentary "Raoni", with music by Egberto Gismonti, narration by Jacques Perrin and Marlon Brando's 10-minute opening, which he insisted on receiving no compensation. Then, in 1990, he directed a new documentary, "Raoni: An Indigenous Around the World in 60 Days", about the trips of the Kayapo leader.

The tour around the world was due in large part to the support of the English singer Sting, who accompanied him through several countries, to which he carried his message of need to preserve the forest and indigenous culture.

Aritana Yawalapiti. Born in 1950, Chief Aritana is the most recognized indigenous cacique among the inhabitants of the Xingu National Park. Even before occupying the position of head of his tribe, Yawalapiti, in 1980, he inspired the soap opera "Aritana", from the extinct TV Tupi, written by Ivani Ribeiro and televised in 1978 and 1979.

He often says that the importance he attributes to the preservation of indigenous customs he learned it as a child in the coexistence with Orlando Villas-Boas. In recent times, he is distressed by the little zeal that the new generations show in front of the traditions of his people. The Kuarup, for example, perhaps the most emblematic ceremony of the Xingu, he says it has been treated as a joke by young people.

The Yawalapiti language, spoken by half a dozen people, is from the Aruak branch, but the young people have spoken the Tupi, learned from the Kamayura tribe, which shares the same village of the Yawalapitis in the south of the Xingu along with the Kuikuro and Mehinako tribes.

What motivated the Villas-Boas brothers to the creation of the Xingu Park was mainly the possibility of preserving the culture of the Amazonian tribes of southern Para and northern Mato Grosso, bringing them to the same area. All the tribes taken to the place were convinced by those brothers to abandon the practice of the war, that before they waged among themselves. Keeping themselves isolated, indigenous communities lost their cultural references in contact with adventurers who only sought to explore those lands in search of minerals and other riches. The idea of creating a national park of the natives, which the Villas-Boas developed under the guidance of Marshal Rondon, was not intended to leave the natives out of civilization, but instead to integrate them into the universal culture without erasing the records of their traditions, expressed in musicality, pictorial art, handicrafts, festivities, spirituality, languages and legends.

This is how Chief Aritana resents the attitude of the new

generations, who present little appreciation for the knowledge of their parents and grandparents. This new reality harms one of the most important patterns of the indigenous tradition, which is respect for the cultural capital of the elders.

The Brazilian Constitution establishes that basic education in indigenous communities should be developed bilingually, in the language of the tribe and in the Portuguese language. Aritana recognizes that the law has not been fulfilled in this point, and also in others, and makes charges to the authorities of the Republic.

Since not everything is perfect, one of the demands he presents is harmful to indigenous communities and probably originates from some romantic intellectual, and it is an idea that would scarcely pass through the sieve of serious men such as Candido Rondon or Darcy Ribeiro. It is a requirement that the government should cede money, but give the indigenous tribes autonomy to hire the doctors and teachers they deem appropriate, instead of, the government itself, sending these professionals. This may seem harmless at first glance, but it is a nonsense. Let us take the state education network of Sao Paulo. It opens a competition for 2,000 math professors and 10,000 candidacies appear. If the exam is well prepared, the top 20% are approved, some of them opting for indigenous community schools. It was like this until the beginning of the 21st century. With that new romantic philosophy, which Aritana embraces without realizing that it comes from wrong people, the indigenous villages of the south of the city of Sao Paulo demanded the Education Department to determine that the vacancies of teachers is filled by Guarani teachers, excluding them from the universe choice of the other teachers. As there were not enough cadres of graduates in the State of Sao Paulo, people from the State of Parana came to fill the vacancies. The teachers became all Guarani, selected in a reduced universe of choice. The result of this is that in the first general examination (Saresp: System of assessment of the regular students of Sao Paulo State) carried out after completion of the measure, the state school Guyra Pepoh ("Bird's Wing"), of the region, was in last place among the five thousand state school units of Sao Paulo. It was a disaster that even the fiercest critic of that "autonomy" would have been able to predict. Of the hundreds of municipalities in the state, none have claimed this autonomy for themselves, because each knows that this would be harmful. It could not be different with the indigenous communities.

But, while engaged in the preservationist struggle, Aritana, as it happened with Raoni, rightfully revolted against the environmental neglect shown by the government in the construction of the Belo Monte Hydroelectric Power Plant. It was not the case to refuse the march of progress, for that would be to disrespect Rondon's memory. The problem is that the Xingu River has undergone substantial intervention without a conversation between the government and the indigenous leaders, who have their orientations and objections to the project of the plant, as well as to other projects.

In 2004 he sent, along with his brother Pirakuman, a message to the indigenist Moacir Melo, asking him to refer it to the president of the Republic at the time. In one passage he said: "We thought you were people! You are the monster that likes to end our forest, our river and our land!" The letter ends with the phrase: "Please, let us work with joy, peace, and caring for Brazil's environmental protection."

Respect for nature is a non-negotiable part of the American native tradition. Darcy Ribeiro said in relation to the natives with whom he lived: "They knew the name of each forest animal, each little herb."

Mario Juruna. Born in 1943 in Barra do Garca, Mato Grosso, and died in 2002 in Brasilia, Federal District, Chief Mario Juruna, from the Xavante tribe, was the first federal representative from Brazil to leave directly an indigenous village. At age 17, he succeeded his father as the head of the tribe and, after meeting the "white man", he began to attend offices in the new federal capital of the country in search of attention to the problems of the natives.

In 1982, having obtained electoral domicile in the State of Rio de Janeiro, he applied for a federal representative for the Labor Democratic Party (PDT), at the insistence of sociologist Darcy Ribeiro and politician Leonel Brizola. While elected with 31,000 votes and speaking Portuguese with an accent of recently contacted Indians, he was initially seen by voters as someone who would not take his term seriously. However, soon the whole country was surprised by his way of negotiating with the authorities of the Executive Power. Always with an audio recorder in tow, all the audiences he got were recorded on his device, because, he explained, he was tired of meeting people who did not keep the word engaged. He created in the National Congress the Permanent Commission of the Indian and denounced, with photos of the money packs, the businessman Calim Eid as he tried to buy his vote for the candidate Paulo Maluf in the congressional election to the presidency of the Republic in 1984.

The indigenous cause, however, did not enchant the Brazilian voters, since the subsequent attempts at election to the same post proved unsuccessful. He did not get elected any more.

He died of diabetes in Brasilia, after being appointed parliamentary aide, and had his body veiled in the National Congress, on July 17, 2002.

Davi Kopenawa Yanomami. Born in 1956, Davi Kopenawa is the main spokesman for his ethnic group, the Yanomami people of northern Brazil. He became internationally known in 1989 upon receiving the *Right Livelihood Award.* After that, he reported in the British and Swedish parliaments that one-third of the Yanomami died between 1959 and 1967, struck by flu and measles epidemics, brought by clandestine prospectors, the first Euro-descendants to contact the tribe. Kopenawa was orphaned early, having lost his father when he was a victim of one of those diseases

He learned to speak Portuguese through evangelical missionaries linked to a United States church. Thus, he became a Funai employee, working as an interpreter. In the 1980s he moved from his original community, in the Toototobi River, to the Watonik village, while marrying there the daughter of the shaman. He soon became head of the Demini indigenous post.

He received the UN 500 Global Award. He then published the book *La Chute du Ciel* (The Fall of Heaven) in France in 2010, in partnership with his French friend Bruce Albert. The book has also been translated and published in English and Portuguese.

Traveling often to other countries, especially in Europe, he continues to denounce the growing invasion of gold miners into the Yanomami lands. It has been charging the Brazilian government for the installation of an indigenous park in the region. In 2014, he revealed that he was receiving death threats from miners.

Marcos Terena. Born in 1954, in the Taunay district of Aquidauana, State of Mato Grosso do Sul, Mariano Marcos Terena was literate in Portuguese at the age of seven. His tribe, Terena, is called Xaneh, by its own members. Marcos Terena is known as "The Aviator Indian", nickname that he also used as the title of one of his books.

Like Juruna, it was also a bet of Darcy Ribeiro and Leonel Brizola as a candidate of the PDT to federal constituent representative in 1986, but without the accent of the newly contacted Indians, he did not have enough exotic appeal to achieve success in the campaign, and not was elected, despite the intellectual preparation he holds.

In fact, as a child, in the first year of primary school, he refused the role of exotic and folkloric animal that they tried to attribute to Indian boys. He perceived the great prejudice that the Euro-descendants showed about him and fought from the beginning against it. He was once called "Japanese", and then discovered the key to personal progress: to blend in with the descendants of the Japanese from Campo Grande and camouflage his indigenous identity, what he did for 14 years. As a "Japanese", he was respected at school and managed to receive adequate instruction in primary school and to enter the city's busiest high school, Campograndense State Secondary School, where he attended high school junior and high school. He passed the Air Force Academy exams and learned how to fly airplanes, becoming a commercial pilot. When he was about to obtain the pilot's license, he faced difficulties, because his indigenous identity was no longer a secret. People from indigenous villages had to be supervised by Funai, and could not be aircraft pilots as ordinary citizens, according to the authorities' understanding. After three years of analysis of his petition, with comings and goings, the Brazilian Air Force authorized the grant of the license, while recognizing his personal merits. He then worked as a Funai jungle pilot.

With his brother, Carlos Terena, he created the Indigenous Peoples Games, an event that brings together the various tribes of Brazil and neighboring countries in sporting competitions, and resulted in the World Indigenous Peoples Games, whose first edition took place in Palmas, State of Tocantins, in 2015, bringing together Aboriginal athletes from various parts of the Earth.

The story of Marcos Terena pretending to be "Japanese" in order to overcome the prejudice against the Indians, which fell in the hand of the author of this book with the present work already in progress and almost finished, came to the thesis defended here: if we had been seen as the Orientals we are, since the arrival of Columbus, Vespucci, Cabral, Cortez and Pizarro, and not as a lost and uncultured branch of Indian descendants, without any demerit to the Indians, who bequeathed us the Hindu-Arabic numerals and the codified religions, if we had been seen us as a branch of Japanese, or Chinese, they would have bet on us as great trading and cultural partners, and we would have had five centuries of progress, instead of five centuries of tutelage.

Ailton Krenak. Born in the Krenak tribe, when it already had some degree of miscegenation with Euro-descendants, in 1953, in the Vale do Rio Doce, State of Minas Gerais, Ailton Alves Lacerda Krenak is a friend of this author for many decades. He is a writer, activist of the indigenous cause and professor at the Federal University of Juiz de Fora, in courses of specialization, of the subjects "Culture and History of Indigenous Peoples" and "Arts and Crafts of Traditional Knowledge".

Those who followed Brazilian politics in the years of the elaboration of the Federal Constitution of 1988 remember his inflamed speech in the tribune of the National Congress, with the face painted with jenipapo ink, denouncing the little case of the parliamentarians and the authorities in general in the consideration rights of indigenous peoples.

In Minas Gerais he created the Nuclei of Indigenous Culture, which, among other activities, is promoting, since 1998, the Festival of Dance and Indigenous Culture, in the municipalities of Serra do Cipo (Liana Mountain).

Evo Morales. Born on October 26, 1959, in the Aymara tribe of Bolivia, Juan Evo Morales Ayma has been president of Bolivia since January 2006. Before being elected by the MAS (Movement for Socialism) party, he had gained notoriety for having, as leader of coca growers, coca farmers, confronted and defeated the United States in the purpose of replacing the planting of that tea in indigenous areas by growing bananas.

It is still suspected that part of the Bolivian coca will be used for the illegal production and export of cocaine, but Evo Morales, during his term, has guaranteed that there will always be "zero cocaine and zero drug traffic, but no zero coca", once the cultivation and use of the plant are an essential part of the Andean culture.

His policy has reduced poverty in the country, but he may smear his biography if he insists on the project of becoming a warlord with his attempts to constitutionally abolish the limit on the number of presidential reelections, as China's Xi Jinping recently did.

Daniel Munduruku. Born in Belem, State of Para, on February 28, 1964, Daniel Munduruku, now living in Sao Paulo, is a professor of Philosophy and a writer, with fifty children's books published.

With a Master's degree in Anthropology and a Doctorate in Education from the University of Sao Paulo, when he is asked whether he is or not an Indian he responds that "Indian is a social invention, a folklore". What he can guarantee is that he descends from the Munduruku tribe and decided to embrace the indigenous cause as an indigenous writer, in opposition to the indigenist writers such as Jose de Alencar and Goncalves Dias, who, he says, have created harmful stereotypes. His first book is called "Indian Stories".

Among the various prizes he received it is a Jabuti trophy, as well as medals of Unesco, the presidency of the Republic of Brazil and the Brazilian Academy of Letters.

Eunice Baia. Born on June 2, 1990, in Barcarena, State of Para, Eunice Barros Baia, a descendant of the Bareh tribe, with a miscegenation pointed after her surname, but carrying indistinguishable native traits, starred at the age of eight the feature film "Taina - An Adventure in the Amazon", directed by Tania Lamarca and Sergio Bloch and released in January 2001. The production selected it in a universe of 3,000 children from all over

Brazil. During the filming, Eunice strongly attached herself to Noemia Duarte, casting director. After the work was finished, she began to cry a lot, telling her parents in Belem, where she lived, that she wanted to go to Sao Paulo to be with her tutor. The parents finally gave in and gave her custody to Noemia, who in Sao Paulo began to treat her as a daughter, referring her to studies and being called "Mamu", the affectionate nickname Eunice invented for her.

Seven years later Eunice performed in Taina II, but by then she had decided that she did not want to continue acting in cinema, because what she liked to do most of all was to draw. She joined the Fashion Design course at the University Center of Fine Arts in Sao Paulo and is a graduate of the area, to which she dedicates herself professionally. She is married and has a small child.

Even though it has decided to move away from the indigenous cause in adulthood, the message of the work "Taina", in defense of the fauna and flora of the Amazon, which she bequeathed to subsequent generations, is a vital document in the history of the Americas. With her Japanese face, her talent and her trajectory, she involuntarily embodies the thesis advocated in this book as few could do.

10.
Conclusion

Examples such as that of Marcos Terena, of indigenous pretending to be Japanese to escape negative discrimination and tutelage, there must be many along the American continent, from Alaska to Tierra del Fuego. It's just a matter of searching and finding.

When the wave of the dekasegis, the Nisseis migrating to Japan, began, to work there and to make some money, it appeared the news that in Peru indigenous were doing plastic surgery in the eyelids to go to work in Japan like descendants of Japanese. Certainly, either case worked.

For us, in the Americas, the great difference of phenotype between indigenous and Japanese is even in the shape of the eyelids. We are from an Eastern branch that had eyes similar to those of Europeans and Africans. And it is for this reason that for five centuries they denied the Asian theory for the origin of the peoples of America, without regard to the work of nineteenth-century historian William Hickling Prescott on Eastern origin, but insisting baselessly on autochthonous theory, which would justify a "red race". Certainly we have darker skin than the Chinese and Japanese, who are called "yellow", but to think that our skin was red demanded a great deal of theorizing.

If, instead of discovered by Europeans at the end of the fifteenth century we had been discovered by Japanese or Chinese, sailing eastward in the Pacific Ocean, we would have been seen by them as their relatives, and our history would have been completely different.

Today autochthonous theory is discarded, and the Asian theory emerges as the only plausible to explain our origin. What we still do not know is which island, or which islands, from the vast Pacific Ocean, we leave, or if we come from the continent, where there are Vietnamese, Koreans, Chinese and Mongols. Anyway, if we came from the islands, those who were on those islands came from the mainland.

We do not yet know whether it is a coincidence that the Tupi-Guarani language, prior to the contamination with the Iberian languages, have developed without the sound of the letter "L", like the Japanese language. Now, the Mapuche, Aruak, Quechua, and North American nations use this letter, as many other smaller tribes do it. And one of the small differences between Tupi and Guarani is that this last has the letter "V", which in the words of Tupi is almost always replaced by "B", as is the case of the word "tierra", which is "yvy" in Guarani and "ibi", or, depending on the region, iuih, in Tupi. Thus, the Tupi, which was the language of almost the entire Brazilian coast, does not have the "V" sound. Exactly like in the Japanese language.

Yes, we are of Eastern origin. However, the idea is not yet embodied in people's behavior. The paradigm of previous centuries, of seeing the natives of the Americas as a lost, backward and poor branch of Indians, from India, remains very strong in the minds. And the "installed base", through governments and laws, is that of tutelage, based on the view that we indigenous people are inferior.

What are we? If we consider the Japanese and the peoples of the continent, Chinese and close relatives, as the first great branch of the Orientals, the peoples of the southernmost islands, such as Filipinos, Indonesians, Malaysians, and also Hawaiians, as the second great branch, then we natives of the American continent are the third great branch.

In an effort to deny citizenship, and therefore isonomy, to the natives, the United States Supreme Court ruled on November 3, 1883, that Native Americans are not... Americans. That decreed they are foreigners, without the right of independence and, consequently, without the right to equality before the law vis-à-vis other citizens of the country in which they were born. And this was not a discretionary act of the court, for years before, on April 1, 1866, the Congress of the country had passed the Civil Rights Law, granting equal rights to persons born in the territory, except for the natives.

In the twentieth century, with previously ignored historical and anthropological knowledge, governments progressed, albeit slowly, towards the extension of indigenous rights. It belongs to this trajectory the "Native American Graves Protection and Repatriation Act", signed by President George Herbert Bush on November 16,

1990. One cannot deny that this law represented a change in the treatment of the former occupants of the land, requiring respect for traditions.

However, even with great progress made on the issue of isonomy, the population and public agents will continue for decades and decades, perhaps centuries, seeing the Indians as dependent, incapable and deserving of tutelage. In the name of scientific truth, it is necessary that campaigns be carried out in order to bury this past of economic and social losses. For we the natives can produce and contribute to the advancement of society if the civilized ones understand that the native tribes can civilize themselves as much as the descendants of Europeans, Africans and Semites, even before they merge, once we are Eastern like the Chinese and Japanese, only separated from them for millennia, long before the establishment of feudalism and the creation of writing.

The Jesuits attempted, in the Reductions, based on the Letter of James ("If you show favoritism with persons, you commit a sin") and in the Letters of Paul, who also condemn "to make favoritism", to raise the natives, through education, art and work. They sought to rescue Christianity from the Neoplatonics, who rejected slavery, contrary to the doctrine that came from the thirteenth century with the incorporation of Aristotle and his assessment that "backward peoples are the ones who liberate their slaves". The wars finally destroyed the Reductions and the Americas resumed, from end to end, their practice of seeing the indigenous as incapable.

Reconded. Indigenous people are usually discrete?

Another oriental feature, in common with the culture of the Japanese, is identified in the attitude of the Caiçaras, the natives of the coast of Sao Paulo who took refuge in the foothills of the Sea Mountain after the defeat of Aimberei against the Portuguese troops in Guanabara Bay in 1557. Many of these villages, as mentioned above, were kept out of contact with Euro-descendants for five centuries, protected from the populations of the Paulista Plateau by the immense barrier that is the Sea Mountain. At the beginning of the 21st century, in islands of the Pacific, some Japanese ex-combatants of the World War II were found, living hidden in the woods for more than 50 years. One of them justified his isolation saying that he believed that the war did not end and that he no longer wanted to participate in any war. It was costly to convince him that the Second War ended in 1945.

Legacy. Did we have influence on the Old World?

By understanding that we are like children, unworthy of exercising citizenship, our rulers, citizens and intellectuals in general have been prevented from perceiving our positive and negative influences on the development of present-day American civilization. And America would be just a transplanted Europe, out of place, if it were not for our Amerindian influences.

On the contrary, through American civilization we have changed the world. Let us look at some of those items of culture that humanity absorbed without awareness of the source.

Federalism. The idea of federation is not an old thing. Today the European Union tries to consolidate itself as a federation, mirrored in the United States and Thomas Jefferson's proposal, since Winston Churchill uttered speech, in 1947, suggesting the creation of the "United States of Europe". Four years later, the European Coal and Steel Community, with six member countries - France, Germany, Italy, Belgium, the Netherlands and Luxembourg - was established as the starting point of what is now the European Union.

In the Old World, before the discovery of America, a union of states had one of the following two origins: or (a) it came from incorporations made by some emperor - such as Cyrus II of Persia, Julius Caesar of Rome, and Genghis Khan of Mongolia -, almost ever by war conquest, or (b) it was formed *ad hoc*, only as a means of facing an external warlike threat, as it was the League of Delos, founded under the guidance of Athens in 478 BC, in order to confront the Persian Empire. The Holy Roman Empire was an attempt by Pope Leo III, when crowning Charlemagne, to establish a great empire, reviving the Roman Empire of the West, through the force of religion, not of armies, but despite having lasted from 800 to 1806, when it was extinguished by Napoleon Bonaparte, the entity never played the role of a truly unified empire, although papal power, not that of the emperors, was the unifying feature of the member states throughout that millennium.

The construction of the concept of federation, as it came to consolidate in the creation of the United States, began with the unions of indigenous tribes engaged in war against the European settlers. At first an incipient federation was formed among the remnants of the Mayan peoples, with their city-states. Mayan culture, already weakened in wars with other indigenous nations, could not sustain this federation for long - there is the alternative hypothesis that the collapse occurred through a long period of drought in the tenth century.

The federation was not a merely warlike union, since it congregated settlements of common language and culture, of Guatemala and of the east of Mexico. The same occurred in the Cunhambebe-Aimberei war, in Rio de Janeiro, when Aimberei, on his own initiative, organized the Tamoios Confederation (1556) among the Tupinamba chiefs of the north of Sao Paulo and the coast of Rio de Janeiro. A few decades later, at the end of that century, the Powhatan chief, Wahunsunacock, created the federation of the Algonquian-speaking natives in eastern Virginia, United States, charging regular tributes from the 30 tribes gathered for the services rendered by the general leadership. When the British landed there in 1607, that federation was already under way.

Later, the Guarani of the Jesuit Missions of southern Brazil and the neighborhoods of Uruguay, Argentina and Paraguay also gathered in federation to confront the Iberians.

However, what inspired Thomas Jefferson in his formulation was the history of the United States itself, surely the federation of the Powhatan chief.

In Brazil, as in other theoretically federated countries, the federation is at risk. The more authoritarian, or plebiscitary, is the doctrinal affiliation of the ruler on duty, more attacks are unleashed against federalism. So, in 2003 a ministry of "cities" was set up to recover streets paving and channel waterways, passing over the mayors of the interior. And in 2018, in addition to the decision to replace the state personal identity document with a national document, a ministry of "security" was also created to override state governors in the management of police work. Whoever thinks the difference between federation and unitary state is irrelevant, should note the fact that the United States, in their two and a half centuries of existence as an independent country, has never fallen into dictatorships. The reason is respect for the federation, because the first measure of a dictator is to abolish the decentralization of power. In the United States they do not convince, although there is a certain degree of unitarianism because of the monetary union, represented in the dollar.

Hospitality. Theoretically, the practice of hospitality is embodied in European civilization. However, the movement of bollards by medieval villages, as well as those with fatal contagious diseases, led to the fortification of the entrances of the households of the families, not only of the palaces. The fear of being attacked by the fellow turned the Europeans distrustful. Among the Semites of Antiquity there was no better situation, as the biblical texts attest. But in America the doors were opened, that is, in stone constructions the doors were vain, with no leaves to open or close. Confidence in the fellowman was almost absolute.

The Europeans, unknown individuals, being received as if they were old friends, took to the Old World the account of how the human species acted when imbued with simplicity and innocence. These aspects have charmed, for example, the French researcher Claude Lrvi-Strauss, former professor of the USP and author of the book "Sad Tropics", among many others. Soon the epidemics spread here, brought by European contagious diseases for which the natives had no antibodies. Indian children died while those of the settlers' sons survived. With no explanation to this fact, several indigenous chiefs rebelled against the immigrants who had been received with open arms. In addition to diseases, greed and the willingness to treat the natives as inferior people, who could be enslaved and protected, were also revealed.

If did not the contagious diseases, and the prejudiced and hostile attitudes - we cannot forget that many adventurers came to America on ships loaded with unsociable and even condemned people -, have occurred, hospitable practice would have been maintained for centuries as a valuable teaching for the settlers.

Balance. While Old World individuals needed Buddhism and Christianity to remind them that we are all equal before the Creator and that, as a consequence, laws should regard citizens as equal in principle, we natives of the Americas have in our behavior the sense of equal treatment and rejection of breach of agreements. The negative discrimination of an indigenous person against another indigenous person committed by a third person is a serious offense. Also the positive discrimination, the privilege, without the axiological merit associated, is unacceptable.

It was, therefore, an aggressive process of the Euro-descendants in relation to the unmixed natives to make them swallow the idea that they have no autonomy, do not deserve to enjoy isonomy in front of other peoples and must be under guardianship. Many of the wars between the natives and the United States Army began precisely in the announcement of the transfer of the tribes to reservations, which represented negative discrimination, protection and isolation, and disrespect for the traditional way of life of those nations.

As for the Guarani War, in the Reductions, the conflict came as a response to the prospect of imminent slavery, since the defense against the Lusophone slayer-hunting Bandeirantes was in the protection that the Spanish crown guaranteed to those communities. Delivering them to the Portuguese yoke, the king of Spain automatically made them prey to the greed of the slavers.

The introjection of symbolic violence apparently occurred, with the Indians accepting tutelage and even negative discrimination. However, what may have occurred was the finding of military inferiority, as did warrior Black Hawk, with a consequent collective attitude of subservience.

If we had been seen as equals, not as incapable children, we could have shown to the Europeans that they should follow the pope in his opposition to slavery. European Christianity, as stated above, while inspired by Plato's ideas, peremptorily rejected slavery, so that by the year 1000, although it tolerated the condition of servitude, it only lived with slavery regimes in the Vikings of Denmark and in the Muslim occupation of the Iberian Peninsula.

The Catholic Church, from its official institution in Rome at the beginning of the fourth century, reproved slavery, although a specific papal document on the subject came to light only in the year 1435, in the *Sicut Dudum* bull of Pope Eugenius IV. Other papal texts followed, including the *In Plurimis* encyclical of Pope Leo XIII, which called on the bishops of Brazil to support Dom Pedro II and Princess Isabel in their decision to abolish slavery in the country. The consolidation of the Christian vision on this ground came in the seventh century with Queen Bathilde, wife of King Clovis II of France. Before she became queen she had been a slave and on the throne instigated the king to pursue without cease the practice of slavery. Yes, the Holy See and the Popes always opposed slavery, but Aristotle, whom the Church accepted in the thirteenth century, found, unlike Plato, that the slave institution was a sign of advancement ("Treaty of Politics"). That is why, during mercantilism, the voice of the papacy was overshadowed, and the slave trade flourished.

In order not to leave the impression that there is an absolute rigidity of the rule of isonomy, it should be remembered that the indigenous culture accepts a natural positive discrimination, which is the ascendancy of the elders. At the opposite extreme, it also accepts the need for child protection. Age discrimination is now being cultivated worldwide, with the understanding that the rights of children, adolescents and the elderly have a distinction in relation to the rights of adults who are members of the economically active population. We "Amerindians" respect the elders in a deeper way than the ancient Semites, the African peoples, and our remote ancestors from the Far East. While we were subjected to numerous weather, death from snake and mosquito bites, drowning, verminoses and many other ills reduced the average life of the forest tribes. Those who reached old age showed signs of being the holder of a natural reward, a blessing from the Great Spirit, or from Tupan. Perhaps this contributed to the great respect raised by the younger ones.

Respect for elders extends to the fellowmen in general, albeit to a lesser degree. The native avoids interfering in the other's way of being. If a native is distressed and wants to put out what torments him, Darcy Ribeiro said in a conversation that this author participated, then he can come out screaming in the village square with the most languishing cries, without causing any irritation or awe in the other persons.

Defects. It is part of the human condition to possess qualities alongside defects. Even if an individual judges himself perfect in his behaviors, for the individuals in his circle of coexistence, part of his arsenal of positive behaviors forms a set of defective practices, such as the very claim to be perfect. As Vilfredo Pareto wrote, disagreeing need is in the natural condition of the human being - he would have classified it as a "defense mechanism" if he had used Freudian terminology. So, if we happen to know a perfect person, then we'll give him a flaw.

Once we are, like all other peoples, imperfect people, we cannot hide our problems, especially because there is a chance of correcting them when we explain them.

That which can be classified as our greatest defect is the consequence of one of our positive qualities, hospitality. It is our *contempt for our compatriots* and their productions. Just as we welcome the foreigner well, at least in the early days, and we greatly value the products they bring, so we unwillingly receive our neighbors in ethnicity, language and customs, and reject their ideas and inventions. The Euro-descendant inhabitants of the United States, who miscegenated very little with the natives, escape this destiny. In the rest of the Americas, we only value the foreigner. If any person, or any community, knows how to appreciate the production of his peers, of the natives, it is because they went through a doctrinal work of conscientization. Otherwise, progress itself is always seen as minor and of little value. A book written in Spain is seen as superior to a book written in Mexico, in the same theme and in the same Spanish language, even when Mexico's is better. The same is true of a cinematographic work, a painting, a sonata or a bicycle.

Another cultural problem of ours is that we do not give importance to the clock, even though it was an apparatus brought by the Europeans, close to the practice of respecting schedules of commitments. We continue to arrive *late* to previously scheduled events, as if this did not cause any losses. The Europeans had been accustomed to clocks since ancient times with sundials, and since the early decades of Alexandria with the hydraulic pointer clock created by Ctesibius. We, on the other hand, did not adapt to this instrument, neither in the beginning, in 1500, nor today, in the years 2000 to now.

The passion for firearms was immediate in the United States. And even though there had been a very small number of marriages between natives and Europeans, that tendency of the Indians in their enchantment by the *pistols* had contaminated the country for a long time. Since the seventeenth century, only in the year 2018 has it started a youth movement to collect restrictions on the use of weapons.

Another custom with dire consequences, though it may seem innocent, is to tell *glib lies*. It is not a story at all, but a fanciful invention. Once again, the people of the United States are the ones who have been most drawn to this practice. Let us recall the preaching of shaman Wovoca, bragging that if the natives enlarged the force and contingent of participation in the ritual of the "ghost dance", the Earth would swallow the Euro-descendants. Seen from all angles, this seems to be a conversation of mentally handicapped people, but many natives allowed themselves to be persuaded by him, including Sitting Bull, who, because of the adhesion, had a tragic end for himself.

Still in the field of crazy lies, we had the teaching of Quanah Parker, one of the leaders of the Native American Church (NAC), repeating that: "The white man goes to church and talks about Jesus, but the Indian goes to the tent and talks with Jesus". Now, the white man turns to Jesus, hoping to be heard. And he talks about Jesus in the church. To pretend to talk to Jesus, even if it happens to one or the other, is not something to be bragged about. But Quanah Parker did not fear ridicule in making that statement. And he inspired religious currents that developed in the twentieth century from that belief. If they did not convince many in the United States, they spread like wildfire in Latin America and other continents.

The old "fisher talk", in which the individual boasts of having caught colossal fish, fantastic animals or unusual objects from the bottom of the water, is one of the traditions that come from those innocent lies. The fact presents no problem when it is delimited to the field of fiction, and must continue being cultivated, even as an exercise in creativity. This is the basis of the "fantastic realism" style of Latin American literature. But the miraculous lies that can cause harm, these must be curtailed and, definitely, abandoned.

Finally, we have to register a very negative trait of our weaknesses: the crush on *distillates* and *tobacco*. When Columbus landed on our beaches in 1492, distilled alcohol had not yet been invented and there was no thing such as whiskey, brandy, or any of these liquid flushes that lead the user to get drunk quickly, and which happened to be called "drink". The distillate did not come to light until 1498 in the Great Britain. But, brought by the settlers, the liquid soon enchanted the natives. They were delivering gold, silver, and diamonds in exchange for this low-value commodity. The colonists also processed the tobacco, traditionally used by the natives, in showy cigarettes, to take to Europe, but they negotiated with the natives also this piece. In Europe, our tobacco has spread as an almost obligatory item of entertainment, so much so that Peter I of Russia, while having learned about it in Holland, upon his accession to the throne forced the counselors to cut the beard, like Western Europeans, and to learn smoking. Today we know that the habit is harmful to health and we try to quell it. But the custom of ingesting distillates, which is much more tragic, remains in force.

Ira Hamilton Hayes was an iconic case. Born in 1923, an Indian of the Pima tribe of Arizona, he was one of the six heroes immortalized in the photo of Joe Rosenthal of the Associated Press, on the hoisting of the United States flag on Mount Iwo Jima, Japan, in World War II, on February 23, 1945.

The six soldiers in the photo were given all the honors that the heroes live up to, becoming celebrities. When sought, years later, for new honors, five of them were located and were well. Hayes, however, the only indigenous person of the group, was indulged in alcoholism. He died the night of January 23 to January 24, 1955, drunk and exposed to the cold. Popular songwriter Peter La Farge paid tribute with the song "Ballad of Ira Hayes", which was recorded by Johnny Cash (listen at **bit.ly/1m6gLJz**).

In Brazil, the Funai pays monthly benefits to many indigenous people. A great part of them spend all they get on the first three or four days of the month with distilled drinks. Alcoholism is a disease, officially recognized by the medicine, and these Indians are victims, as if they were victims of any other epidemic. The romantics reject criticism of the use of public benefits for the purchase of distillates, but they are the same ones who want to "spare" the Indians from being attended by professors and doctors selected in the wide Euro-descendant universe.

It's time to do something about it. One way is to strictly prohibit the purchase of distillates by persons over the age of 21, freeing it for persons aged 16 to 20, with a fine for violators. Such a move reverses the traditional policy of linking the freedom to drink alcohol to mature people and the goal is to overturn the glamour of the business. If it is an article just released for adolescents, the reading that responsible citizens have to do is that to be an adult it is necessary to escape from that. The total ban, for all age groups, as in the United States Dry Law, does not work, as we already know, since dependents will pay any price to get the product, in clandestine hands.

Perspectives. Does the use of the Pacific-centered *mappa mundi* have any advantages?

This view of the ban on adult distillates is one of the possibilities among measures to be taken to improve the lives of indigenous people. In this case, to improve the life of society in general.

Let us then speak about suggestions that can reverse the sad fate of the native peoples of the Americas as painted today.

Map. As Eastern origin, and linked to the Pacific Ocean, we were accustomed from an early age, and for centuries, to read the planisphere, the *mappa mundi* printed on paper, designed for Europeans, with Western Europe and the Atlantic Ocean at the center. Countries in the Far East use the other side of the map, seeing it with the Pacific Ocean in the center, Asia to the left and America to the right of the eye.

The first practical demand for this book is therefore the use of the eastern map, with the Pacific Ocean in the center, to be used in schools of indigenous communities, both in South America and in Central and North America. This will always remind us of where we came from, in order to increase self-esteem and pride in the condition of Eastern descendants. Over time, the Pacific-centered plan could be adopted in schools of Euro-descendants throughout the Americas, alongside the western planisphere. And there will be no cultural loss if we adopt the eastern planisphere definitively, leaving the West to Europeans and Africans. This does not mean that America becomes part of the East. We will continue Western, but aware of Eastern origins.

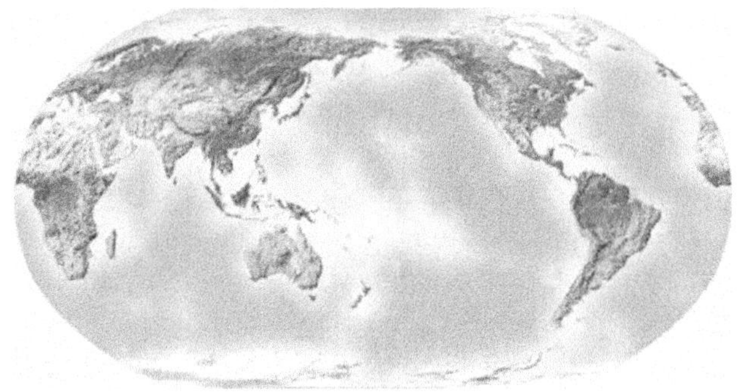

Pacific-centered *mappa mundi*

The adoption of the map is a beginning of a change of consciousness, but alone can have no practical effects. Knowing that the ethnic group is connected to the Chinese and Japanese is not enough to guarantee a new reality. The Hazara ethnic group in Afghanistan can be taken as an example. It is a group clearly related to the Chinese, who are nearby. However, until the overthrow of the Taliban's dictatorial government in 2001, this group suffered discrimination comparable to that of the indigenous peoples of the Americas. Hazaras could not enter higher education and could not be part of the public service, with an even greater burden of restrictions on women. Now, in the democratic regime, even though it is incipient, the opening has come to those people, who, finally, have citizen status.

Ministry. In each country of the Americas, the Ministry of Education should instruct its primary school teachers to see in each native child a relative of Kurosawa, Mutsuhito, Yoko Ono, Basho, Tomie Ohtake, Deng Xiao Ping, Confucius, Lao Tzu and Ban Ki-moon, that is, to see him as a descendant of Eastern peoples as much as these quoted names are.

The self-fulfilling prophecy that has settled on each teacher's mind in these five centuries of misguided view of the natives needs to be reversed. It had previously predicted that indigenous boys are inferior, incapable and destined for tutelage by the public power. From this beginning of the millennium, it should be borne in mind that, just as the peoples of the Far East have grown spectacularly in the field of education in recent times, so too their "indigenous" relatives can grow and raise the Americas to a much higher level than the current one on the world scenery. The "Pygmalion effect", or "Rosenthal effect", must now embody the perspective that boys will be great musicians, great painters, great readers, great engineers, great doctors, great paramedics, great teachers, great aviators, great civil servants, great entrepreneurs, great operators of industrial machines, great communicators, great farmers, great economic agents and great professionals in any activity that society demands.

Such a campaign should be done in printed texts, face-to-face lectures, videos and all possible forms of communication.

And we have to deny the request of Chief Aritana, about granting autonomy to the indigenous communities to choose doctors and teachers, because this idea of romantic exclusivism is not something indigenous, but evil planted in their minds by deceivers, demagogic enemies of the cause of the natives.

Spokesperson. The National Foundation of the "Indian" - Funai, in Brazil - and its equivalents in the other countries of America must have as presidents people originating from the native tribes, as long as they hold formal education in line with the position. It must be so because, however much a "white" scholar of the cause has knowledge and commitment, he did not absorb in childhood the core of the culture of these peoples. However, the second position in the hierarchy of the foundation must be occupied by a indigenist of

European or African ancestry. The position is as a spokesperson, or public relations, but with a comprehensive approach, starting with the role of firebreaker, not to prevent Europeanizing customs from reaching native communities, but to avoid, by persuasion and information, that cultural traditions of the tribes are no longer valued by young people and are lost in the inevitable tangle of data acquisition that openness to the world brings. Chief Aritana complaint about adolescents' contempt for traditional indigenous culture is clear evidence that the treasurer of the legitimate values of ancestry must be someone from outside the community. Aritana needs a professional like Orlando Villas-Boas today, and the public power must take care of naming this agent, in a position of prominence. The contracted indigenists exist, with their competences, but it is necessary to give inauguration to this special figure, who is the spokesperson of the Foundation.

Eastern. The following suggestion is implemented through approval in national parliaments. This is the establishment of the "*eastern cities*". First, small or medium-sized indigenous reservations become indiscriminately "*reservation-municipalities*", with prefects elected for four-year terms and with the entire structure of common municipalities, even if they maintain the functions of cacique and shaman. A very large reservation, such as the "Raposa Serra do Sol", or a national indigenous park, such as the Xingu, these are divided into several reservation-municipalities, according to the geographic layout of the villages.

An "eastern city" is a reservation-municipality that opts for the emancipation of its inhabitants, with the abolition of all official guardianship over adult individuals. The children receive from the government the same treatment that the children receive from the non-indigenous municipalities of the country, with the difference that the teachers who there work are instructed by the education authorities to look at the students as promising branches of the descendants of Extreme East peoples, embracing this liberating spirit. They will continue, as in other reservations, to receive instruction in the native language of the tribe and in the official language of the country, but will be seen as boys preparing for an emancipated adult life, citizens, not individuals protected. Certainly, in order to become "eastern city" the reservation-municipality must rely on prepared leading cadres, with at least complete secondary education.

In just one more aspect, the "eastern cities" are distinguished from the ordinary municipalities of the country: they receive the attention of the member states, as expected, but also receive special attention from the federal power in the first decades of existence, the first 50 years, for example. The condition is not perpetual to avoid attacking federalism. And to those who imagine that this special attention can lead to a new form of guardianship, it is explained that there will be no guardianship over individuals and that these cities should be seen as diamond to be lapidated, which is never more at the mercy of greedy miners or inconsequential governments.

In the "Indigenous Peoples' Games" these "eastern cities" will continue to participate, as well as in indigenous congresses or in any other activities that concern native peoples. What differentiates these people from the other natives is the fact that they are emancipated, regular citizens of the country.

Brazil already has a regular municipality, Tacuru ("Termite"), in Mato Grosso do Sul, which has the Guarani language as an official language, alongside Portuguese. Throughout the municipality there is a recommendation that both languages be taught in schools. Tacuru could become the first "eastern city" in Brazil. Paraguay, which has Guarani as one of the official languages of the country, can declare as "eastern city" a very large number of municipalities. Many municipalities in Bolivia and Peru may also be declared "eastern cities", but one should not forgot that the current reservations are the ones that should be in the forefront of this policy in the first place.

The "eastern cities" do not constitute identity politics, contrary to what some unsuspecting person may come to imagine. Who does this is the policy of reservations of protected people, which has been postponing, perhaps for the next millennia, the transformation of the natives into full citizens.

In the municipal areas of the "eastern city" one should not abolish the concept of community ownership of land cultivated in the old reservations. The most auspicious policy will be to restore the system that the Jesuits created in the Missions: communal land

(Tupambaeh) in most of the territory and family farm (avambaeh), as private property, to a small extent, for each family that wants a proper place of culture. It is a farm of 9 hectares (equivalent to 300x300 m²) at most, which is an area that a family man can weed. In the communal land the inhabitants of the "eastern cities" will be able to practice sustainable development and environmental preservation, according to their tradition.

Clearly visible progress of the citizens of the "eastern cities" will lead the remaining reservations to seek the authorities and propose adherence to the program.

However, let us not feed the belief that there will be 30 Marcos Terena in every ninth-grade classroom. There will be three in 30, as in China, India, Nigeria, Italy or Canada. It is the proportion among heuristic students, 10% of the class, and the total, which is completed by 90% of sensitive students. Those first ones are the ones who elaborate their answers in the examinations, whereas these 90% are those who memorize the contents. If we forbid them from memorizing matter, as we have done since 1952, their output will be to copy responses from heuristics if the system is relaxed, what means brutal havoc in the education of youth. The policy of preventing pure and simple *memorization* is far worse than that of requiring it for all, though one should not go back to it ever again, for harming heuristics in this way means overthrowing the bulwarks of society as well as the practice of abandonment of evaluation, or respect for merit. Thus, the natural candidates for the position of class representatives should be the three students, maxime four, of *higher school performance* in the room, attested in their bimonthly marks. The class should be called to vote and choose among these names. Those who do not win in the first place occupy the positions of first-vice, second-vice, etc., in order to guarantee the continuity of their encouragement to studies. Suffraging the names of the most well-evaluated is not undemocratic because the system presupposes mobility: one who is below in the present year can grow and reach the top the following year, either with "Vieira's crack" or with a different dedication to studies. The elect may thus be both a heuristic and a sensitive. In the last grade of high school, the application is open to all students in the class, once they will already be accustomed to choosing scholars. Only those who are repeating the school year, who do not represent the majority, are vetoed.

The investment, we should warn, will have a very small and very slow gain if the scholastic teaching is not abandoned. In the case of Brazil, it was reestablished in 1971 by the military regime, with the untying between the school and the world of work. The political model of the Louis-Bonapartist presidential election, adopted by Mexico in 1857 and followed today throughout Latin America, must also be abandoned, unless a larger organizational structure is created, because it destroys any effort for the quality of basic education.

The *vocational* high school is the only configuration that makes sense at this level of schooling, and to institute it is very easy, with just the courage and understanding to make the decision. All high school courses that are not technical, and that today are almost all, begin to adopt the curricular matrix of *commercial course*. How to do it? A new subject matter, *Accounting Economics*, of two weekly classes, enters the schedule grid. In the first year, the subject is Accounting. In the second, Microeconomics (never Macroeconomics, which is the subject of postgraduate students). Finally, in the third year, Finance. In the case of the Brazilian curriculum, Art Education in the first year is replaced by this new subject (taught by teachers of Mathematics, Physics, Geography or others), because the idea of Arts in the first year of high school came to contemplate the entrance of Music, of Villa-Lobos's plan, which covered four junior years plus a year in high school, and the subject was completely abolished by the military regime. Music should come back, but it does not have to go through high school.

Investment and vision change are all the more necessary if one grows aware that there is a historical debt. It is not a pecuniary debt, as many defend in relation to the descendants of slaves, but a litigation, still dormant, because of the treatment that the Europeans and their American descendants gave to the natives, when, because they were endowed with more advanced technology than the one from here they were judged to be superior beings and, under the erroneous conception of the "lost Indian", they treated as incapable the tribes they met in the New World. This debt covers the moral, intellectual and political aspects.

If the reader, after reading this book, sees the Amerindians from a positively different view, then the central goal of having written it was fulfilled.

@cacildo
cacildomarques@gmail.com